Walk!

The

Lake District South

with

Charles Davis

DISCOVERY WALKING GUIDES LTD

Walk! The Lake District (South)
First Edition - January 2006
Copyright © 2006

Published by
Discovery Walking Guides Ltd
10 Tennyson Close, Northampton NN5 7HJ,
England

Mapping supplied by **Global Mapping Limited**
(www.globalmapping.com)

This product includes mapping
data licensed from **Ordnance Survey®** with the
permission of the Controller of Her Majesty's
Stationery Office. © Crown Copyright 2005. All rights
reserved.
Licence Number 40044851

Photographs
All photographs in this book were taken by the
author, or by Jeanette Tallegas.

Front Cover Photographs

Side Pike, on Walk 15

On Walk 9,
Yewbarrow

Chapel Stile (Walk 14)

**Above Stanley Gill with Sca
Fell in the background
(Walk 4)**

ISBN 1-904946-16-X

Text and photographs* © Charles Davis

Walk!
The Lake District South

CONTENTS

THE WALKS

A ESKDALE and THE SOUTHWESTERN FELLS

B WASDALE

C DUNNERDALE

D GREAT LANGDALE

Charles Davis was born in London, and has lived and worked in the United States, Sudan, Turkey, Ivory Coast, Spain and France. With the onset of middle age, he realised that the urge to roam was better satisfied by walking than bouncing about on the back of a lorry in the middle of the desert, and now divides his time between mountain tops, desk-tops and laptops. He is the author of numerous highly praised and wholly unpublished novels.

Jeanette Tallegas has spent thirty odd years labouring for the French education system, from which she has finally, gleefully, taken early retirement. Asked what she intends doing now, she resolutely replies, "Nothing". Nonetheless, she does follow the author up various gruelling mountains, frequently alarming younger walkers who seem to assume that remote and inaccessible places are the preserve of youth. Charles Davis is also the author of:-

34 Alpujarras Walks   ISBN 1-899554-83-1

Walk! La Gomera (2nd Edition)   ISBN 1-899554-90-4

Walk! Mallorca (North & Mountains)
              (2nd edition)   ISBN 1-904946-19-4

Walk! Mallorca West   ISBN 1-899554-98-X

Walk! La Palma   ISBN 1-904946-06-2

Walk! Andorraa   ISBN 1-904946-04-6

Walk! Axarquía   ISBN 1-904946-08-9

- published by **Discovery Walking Guides Ltd.**

ACKNOWLEDGEMENTS
Ros and David Brawn (of DWG) for the road home, Frank Westcott and Vivienne Crow for suggestions on how to use it, Jeannette for reminding me which side to drive on. Thanks also to Jim, who displayed an appreciation for a faceful of hail that went well beyond the call of friendship, and to Mark and Catherine, for the invention of the trivet and conjuring The Keeper of the Queen's Rabbits.

INTRODUCTION

THE LAKE DISTRICT AND THE FINE ART OF WALKING

The Lake District is to leisure walking what Vienna is to the waltz, Venice to canalization, Bletchley to code-breaking, Chicago to the blues, and Dublin to the brewing of porter. None of these places invented the related pursuit, but in each the activity was honed to a fine art.

Nowadays, our passion for wild places is so widespread it seems innate, but it only really evolved as a popular ideal in the eighteenth century, when a growing appreciation of the picturesque and the increasing security of the English countryside made walking in an undomesticated environment fashionable for the first time. And the place where this new fashion found its fullest expression was the Lake District.

Kirk Fell & Great Gable

With superb lakes carved into spectacularly sculpted valleys, long rugged ridges blessed with imposing panoramas, jagged crags dangling from grand peaks, sweeping dales cradling remote hamlets, and barren fells tonsured with arcane henges and ancient ruins, the Lake District had everything the dedicated wilderness seeker could desire.

It was this 'wilderness' that attracted poets like Thomas Gray, who published the first book about the region in 1775, Coleridge, who made the first recorded ascent of England's highest summit (**Scafell Pike**) in 1802, and of course Wordsworth, who is said to have clocked up some 180,000 pedestrian miles, in the course of which he helped transform walking from an irksome necessity into an enviable indulgence.

Sca Fell from Lingmell

For Wordsworth, walking was literally poetry in motion, most of his poems being composed as he walked, but it was also a means of escaping the social and political constraints of his age. Anyone who has since walked to get away from the clatter and clutter of the workaday world, is following in his footsteps.

Some of the trails the Romantic poets enjoyed are now under tarmac, others are so heavily used their charm is marred, but the grandeur and beauty of the landscape are undiminished, and it's still possible to hike in isolation on seemingly untamed land amid vistas that would wring a poem from the most prosaic spectator.

So if you think walking is more than a means of getting from A to B, if you like using your body to traverse terrain that is breathtaking in more than a merely respiratory sense, if you want to wash your mind of the commonplace cares that accumulate in the course of everyday living, if roaming over empty fells under a sprawling sky seems like a grand way of engaging with life, if you want a world that's a little wider than the one you normally encounter... if, in short, you enjoy the fine art of walking, the Lake District is the place for you.

ON THE PAGE: USING THE BOOK

The Lake District is essentially a massive volcanic dome fissured by tectonic pressure then sculpted by glaciation to create a spray of valleys and dividing ridges radiating from a central hub like the spokes of a wheel. There are eleven valleys, sixteen lakes, and 315 'mountains', 170 of them over 2,000ft (610m, the defining height for a mountain in the Encyclopaedia Britannica), four over 3000ft (914m, the only four of this height in England). The **aim of this book** is to provide an outline for a preliminary exploration of the major summits, ridges and valleys in the southern region of the Lake District.

As a **structuring device**, I've grouped itineraries round a pub/B&B/campsite base, on the assumption that most visitors will be taking three to five day breaks and will want to spend as little time as possible in the car. For each base, I've aimed to include the classics, plus a selection of less celebrated and therefore less crowded itineraries. I've also tried to include at least one low level walk in each area that would be feasible in bad weather.

For each walking region I've included a brief **area introduction** outlining points of special interest and accommodation options. Space precludes detailing 'wet day' options but in such circumstances you will find the local tourist offices awash with advice from the helpful staff and more free leaflets on the local attractions than you can shake a walking pole at.

As a rule, the walks within each section are featured in **ascending order of difficulty**, the first being suitable as a test walk or in bad weather, the last a longer more challenging itinerary.

To help assess the nature of a walk, each itinerary is prefaced by a brief introduction and a **rating guide** detailing exertion, walking time, distance, ascents and descents, refreshments, and access.

Timings are all 'pure' timings excluding the rich variety of distraction and lethargy that can extend the simplest walk almost indefinitely. Hardened peak-baggers will regard my timings with withering disdain, but everyone else should allow an extra 15 minutes per walking hour for snacking, snapping and standing still staring. The timings are recorded to the minute but should be treated as an approximate guide. There's nothing more frustrating than walking at someone else's speed, be it faster or slower than your own - so take *your* time and ignore mine if it doesn't match.

Exertion ratings are subjective. Do an easy walk first then judge the rest accordingly.

Hopefully, **refreshment** ratings are more objective, but there's no accounting for taste, so bear in mind that my criteria may not match your own.

Unless stated otherwise, **accommodation** suggestions aren't recommendations premised on a thorough testing of the services, but prompts to be taken up according to need. Bear in mind that the Lake District is *very* popular. Don't leave booking too late, especially in the summer and on Bank Holiday weekends. There are times when the only way you can get a bed is to buy a house.

ON THE GROUND: MAN AND THE LANDSCAPE

Like any rugged landscape, the mountains cradling the Lake District were a barrier to human incursion, but it's a long time since the region was really a wilderness. Even when civilization was at its most rudimentary, these mountains were worked and shaped by man, and the 'wildness' we enjoy today is heavily compromised.

Langdale Pikes from Crinkle Crags

Had man not intervened, the mountains would be mantled in a cloak of oak, birch and pine above which only the highest peaks would be visible, and the valleys would be impenetrable swamps picketed with alder and dense sedges. Instead, we have expansive moor and pasture, partitioned by dry-stone walling, and sprinkled with well-defined lakes and reservoirs.

Given the rich variety of rock and ore in the region, it was perhaps inevitable that quarrying and mining should have been among the first activities to have an impact. Neolithic man fashioned ax and spear heads at **Great Langdale**, the Romans extracted copper from the **Coniston Fells**, and many subsequent generations bored, drilled, dug and hacked their way through the mountains, scarring the landscape with excavations and spoil heaps, and leaving behind a complex of mine buildings, sinkholes, levels, dams and leats.

Climbing to Seathwaite Tarn

The forests meanwhile were cleared as grazing land for the sheep that were vital to medieval England's wealth, or cut back for ships' timbers, bobbins for textile mills, and fuel for smelting iron ore. And as if to confirm man's dominance, the exposed fells have been laced with a web of trails and ways, including Roman roads, peat roads, 'Corpse' or 'Coffin' Roads connecting hamlets to consecrated graveyards, sheep walks, drovers' tracks, packmen's trails, and mining paths.

Nowadays, sessile oak dominates on dry ground, while the damp is dotted with birch and alder. There are also holly, cherry, crabapple, rowan, witch-hazel, yew, beech (the copper beech are particularly impressive) and the ubiquitous Scots pine, though pine and spruce are currently being cleared in many areas in the hope that native broadleaf will return. Juniper was also widely planted as its charcoal was used by gunpowder mills. Outlying areas are best for dendrophiles, especially in some of the less celebrated valleys, where well-managed woodland incorporates some superb oak and a remarkable variety of conifers.

Wildflowers are limited, but one can see wood anemone, asphodels, red campion, lady's mantle, bog myrtle, spotted orchids, saxifrage, stonecrop, saw-worth and thrift - and, of course, the odd daffodil. Though hardly the rarest of displays, bluebells and primrose are particularly fine in outlying woodland during spring, while bracken clad slopes at the foot of higher mountains are often bejeweled with magnificent foxgloves.

Despite human interference, the Lake District remains relatively rich in birdlife, the higher fells providing a seasonal or permanent home to wheatear, ring ouzel, ravens, buzzards, peregrines and a solitary Golden Eagle, while the valleys shelter chaffinch, woodpeckers, nuthatch, sparrowhawks, redstart, pied flycatcher and tree pipit. And with so many lakes and streams, there are plenty of waterfowl, notably goosander, goldeneye, sandpipers, dippers, and wagtails.

Though sightings of otter are reported, mammals are generally the commonplace countryside fauna - fox, hare, stoat, deer, badger, voles, shrews...

Nobody's 'fool'

More noteworthy than wild animals are the sheep, which are everywhere and strikingly varied. As far as walkers are concerned, they often function as purveyors of comic relief, popping their heads up in puzzlement as you approach and barreling off in panic at an unexpected encounter. But according to one anecdote (possibly apocryphall) these flustered creatures are no fools.

You'll notice many gated roads in the Lake District, a consequence, it is said, of sheep belying their dim reputation and learning to roll over cattle grids.

One local word would appear to confirm this fugitive mentality. 'Wratchers' are sheep so sure the grass is greener on the other side of the fence they will scale any obstacle to get a nibble of the neighbours' graminae. By analogy, a married man with a wandering eye is said to be 'a right wratcher'.

Local words are also a useful way of approaching a landscape and the **toponymy** of the Lake District reveals much about its history and individuality. Looking at a map of the area, you will see a pattern of affixes and root words, suggesting a landscape defined by language long before the Romantics began waxing lyrical.

Place names ending with -ton, -ham, -ington indicate a seventh century Anglian community. Scandinavian settlements from the ninth and tenth centuries carry suffixes like -beck, -booth, -fell, -gill, -slack, and -thwaite, while Norse words are also at the root of Greta (Coleridge's Keswick residence - *griot à* a rocky or gravelly river), Ullswater (Ulf's Lake), Ambleside (Hamel's Saetre or farm), and Birkrigg (birch ridge). This process of claiming the land by naming it has continued on a more minute scale into the modern age with the growing popularity of mountain-climbing, as a result of which there are now places where even individual handholds and cracks in the rocks have been named.

The singularity of the Lake District is also reflected in its topographical terms. Other regions have hills and downs, but the Lake District has 'fells' defined by Chambers as "an upland tract of waste, pasture or moorland". Likewise gill (also spelled ghyll) and beck, which both mean brook (beck is cognate with German *bach*), though a gill can also be a small wooded ravine. A tarn (Old Norse *tjörn*) is a small generally remote mountain lake, force (ON *fors*) is a waterfall, moss (ON *mŷr-r*) a bog, hawse (ON *hals*) a neck or col, how (ON *haug-r*) a hill, while *rigg* equates with ridge, -thwaite indicates a woodland clearing, scar and scree come from Old Norse words for cliff and landslip, and keld means a spring, well, or deep still water in a river. And as in all British mountains, there's a strong Gaelic influence, intensified here by the proximity of Scotland and evident in words like burn, corrie, and coombe. Obviously, this lexicon is not unique to the Lake District, but it does constitute a distinct Lakeland vocabulary.

UNDER THE WEATHER: LONELY AS A CLOUD?

"I wandered lonely as a cloud..."

It's a grand line of poetry, economically evoking one of the great pleasures of walking, but as a piece of reportage, it's pretty flabby stuff. Either that or Wordsworth was a strikingly convivial hiker, because if there's one thing clouds aren't in the Lake District, it's lonely. Great gregarious gangs of the things come gamboling in from the Irish Sea, and any cloud looking for solitude would have to be very quick off the mark indeed. There's no point pretending otherwise. If you come to the Lake District, expect to get wet.

That said, seldom will an entire day be spoiled and it will be even less frequent that a full weekend is fraught with bad weather. It's just useful to look on the bright side and hope that it's going to be fine several times a day.

If you're properly equipped, the climate need not be a problem. The most vital piece of equipment is information. Always phone the recorded forecast (0870 0550 575) before setting out for the high fells and opt for a low level walk if bad weather is imminent. The folk providing the forecast are far too chary of Lake District weather to hazard as to what might happen beyond the next 24 hours, which is regrettable when you want to plan ahead. For a general long distance regional forecast, phone 0905 5140003 and select region 09.

This is always a slightly dreary section of a book rehearsing **the dos-and-donts**, but even for experienced walkers, it's worth reminding yourself that a mountain outing can be made miserable or dangerous by lack of planning.

There are many **types of path** in the Lake District, ranging from broad, paved trails to 'ways' defined solely by the fact that some solitary lunatic has taken that route some time in the distant past. A salutary reminder of what some people consider fun comes from Coleridge's journal for August 1802, in which he describes with evident relish his technique for descending **Broad Stand** to the east of the **Scafells**.

Unwilling to waste time finding an easy way down, Coleridge pointed himself in the right direction and set off, "with tolerable ease", until midway down he encountered a seven foot drop. So he just "dropped down". In a few yards, he came to another giant's step and "dropped that, too", and then another and another, at least one being twice his height and ending on a narrow ledge. After a while, he wondered whether it wouldn't be wiser to go back to the top, but having yet to master the technique of dropping up, he was obliged to carry on dropping down, eventually reaching the bottom via the cleft called 'Fat Man's Agony'. This is by no means unique as a Lakeland experience and the chances are you'll encounter at least one 'dropper' during your stay.

Personally, I'm too fond of my knees to countenance too much dropping, but it should be emphasized that much of the walking described here is off path. The popularity of the region means few itineraries are not marked in some manner by the passing of previous hikers, but it's best to read the description in advance, so you know what manner of walk you're taking on. It should also be noted that sheep have made their mark as well and few trails will be free of a confusing array of intersecting sheep-walks.

Equipment is equally important to a pleasurable outing. Coleridge used to set off for a three day walking tour wearing a great coat and carrying a spare pair of socks in his pocket. He also had a heavy laudanum habit, which may go some way to explaining his 'dropping' technique, but is not otherwise recommended. By the same token, 'socks-in-pockets' is not an adequate response to the question of what to take.

Snow shower on Crinkle Crags

Doubtless you'll see the odd fell-runner wearing little more than an exiguous nylon pelmet and an upmarket string vest, but the ordinary walker should always have the means to make themselves wind and water proof, even in the height of Summer. Most people will carry a warm top (jumper or fleece), a windcheater, and a cape or impermeable jacket.

Always take **basic rations**, even if you don't intend picnicking. Ordinarily Kendal mint cake calls for a sugar addiction of daunting dimensions, but it might be just the ticket for the extra energy required in an emergency. For a tooth that's less sweet, dried fruit, cereal bars, high-fibre biscuits and the like are recommended. But whatever your tastes, take something with you every time.

Emergency equipment tends to reflect the degree of optimism of any given walker. Many experienced mountaineers recommend taking a whistle (the distress signal is six blasts repeated at 1 minute intervals), others suggest a bin bag or space blanket in case you have to stay out overnight. I recommend a torch, since there's nothing so painstaking as coming down a mountain in the dark with only a cigarette lighter to show you the way. A torch, flashed at the same 6/1 pattern, can also be used as a distress signal. A mobile phone is not an adequate substitute for basic safety precautions.

Though often ignored, **the basic rule**, "Tell someone where you're going", has to be repeated. The unspoken rider is, "Phone that someone if there's a change of plan". Rescue parties do not delight in the news that the 'missing' walker they've been searching for on windswept fells was actually lost in a pint down the pub.

Finally, stick to the **Countryside Code**. The main change in the new code, revised 2004, brings theory into line with sensible practice, changing the old rule about always shutting gates to leaving them as you found them.

ON THE ROAD: GETTING THERE & GETTING ABOUT

The Wasdale Road

Driving in the Lake District can be delightful or dismal, depending on how many other people are doing it at the same time as you. On weekdays out of season, a private car is the most versatile way of getting around, but in Summer and on Bank Holiday weekends it can be a liability. The **Hard Knott** and **Wrynose** passes are particularly notorious bottlenecks. By choosing bases near the itineraries, we've reduced the need to use a car to the minimum.

If you're visiting for the day, bear in mind that **parking** is often limited. Such strictures notwithstanding, it must be said that even at the busiest of times there are some delightful deserted drives on back roads in outlying areas

For a full guide to national and local **public transport**, see www.traveline.org.uk. You can also telephone Traveline (0870 608 2608), but if you're calling from a fixed line, dial 141 first to avoid being put through to your local information centre. The best place to stay if you're relying on public transport is **Ambleside**.

The nearest mainline **train stations** to our area are **Lancaster** and **Oxenholme**. Branch lines follow the coast from **Lancaster** and go to **Kendal** and **Windermere** from **Oxenholme**. There is a direct train from **Manchester** to **Kendal**. Journey time from **London** is 3h55, from **Manchester** 1h40.

National Express buses (www.nationalexpressgroup.com) connect **London** to **Kendal**, **Ambleside** and **Windermere**.

All areas featured here though not all walks are, in theory at least, **accessible by public transport**. In practice, access to some areas may be seasonally restricted, or the bus service infrequent. That said, it must be emphasized that **Cumbria** has one of the best rural bus services in the country and the advantages of using it will rapidly become apparent when you're searching for a parking space at the start of one of the more popular walks on a busy weekend or fumbling about for enough change to feed the meter. An essential piece of equipment, even if you're arriving by car, is the excellent **Lakesrider** magazine, detailing **Stagecoach** (www.stagecoachbus.com) services throughout the northwest. The magazine is available in tourist information offices.

Mountain Goat minibuses (0153 9445161) link **Grizedale**, **Hawkshead** and **Coniston** at weekends and during the Summer. The service, which is cycle-friendly, is coordinated with the **Bowness** ferries and ties in with a series of walks, outlined in the free B4 (Boat, Bus, Bike & Boot) leaflet, which also includes a detailed timetable.

Day-trippers may wish to consider a public transport day pass, available from local service providers and tourist offices. There are various options combining train, bus and boat, among them the **Lakes Day Tripper** tickets (08457 484950) which provide combined bus/train services to **Windermere** from stations in the Northwest. All bus and boat options are detailed in the **Lakesrider** magazine mentioned above.

If you're having difficulty finding **accommodation**, try www.lakelandgateway.info/booking or phone for B&B/hotels at 0153 9434901, self-catering on 0153 9488785, or the Cumbria Tourist Board Accommodation Booking Hotline on 0808 1008848.

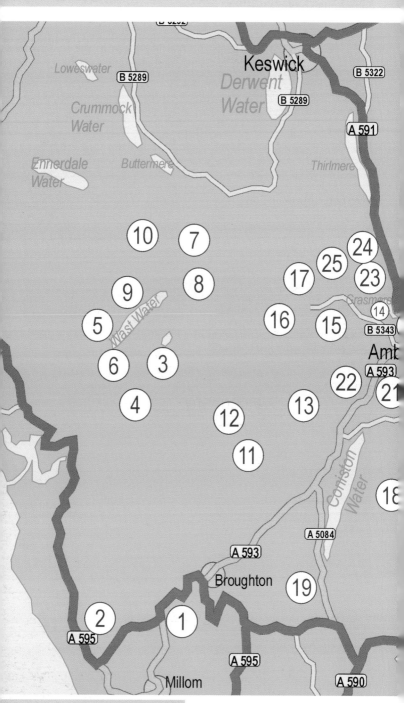

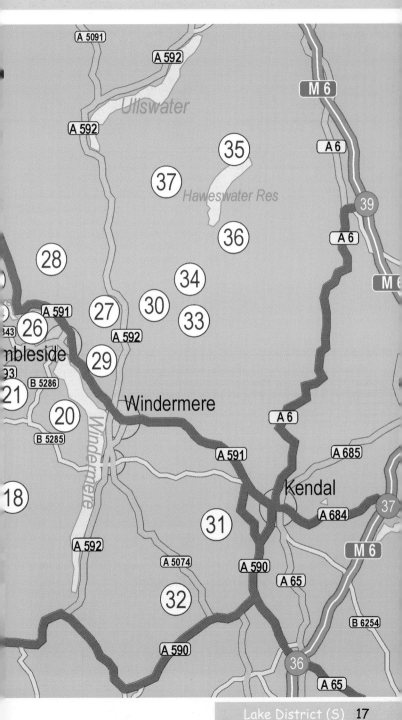

SYMBOLS RATING GUIDE

 3 our rating for effort/exertion:-
1 very easy **2** easy **3** average
4 energetic **5** strenuous

 approximate **time** to complete
a walk (compare your times
against ours early in a walk) -
does not include stopping time

 approximate walking
distance in
miles/kilometres

 250m approximate
ascents/descents in
850m metres (N=negligible)

 circular route   **linear** route   **figure of eight** route   risk of **vertigo**

 refreshments (may be at start or end of a route only)

- Walk descriptions include:
- timing in minutes, shown as (40M)
- compass directions, shown as (NW)
- heights in metres, shown as (1355m)
- GPS waypoints, shown as (Wp.3)

Notes on the text
Place names are shown in **bold text**,
except where we refer to a written
sign, when they are enclosed in single
quotation marks. Local or unusual
words are shown in *italics*, and are
explained in the accompanying text.

ORDNANCE SURVEY MAPPING

All the map sections which accompany the detailed walk descriptions in
Walk! The Lake District South are reproduced under Ordnance Survey
licence from the digital versions of the latest Explorer 1:25,000 scale maps.
Each map section is then re-scaled to the 40,000 scale used in DWG's
Walk!/Walks series of guide books. Walking Route and GPS Waypoints are
then drawn onto the map section to produce the map illustrating the detailed
walk description.

Walk! Lake District South map sections are sufficient for following alongside
the detailed walk descriptions, but for planning your adventures in this region,
and if you to divert from the walking routes, we strongly recommend that you
purchase the latest OS Explorer maps.

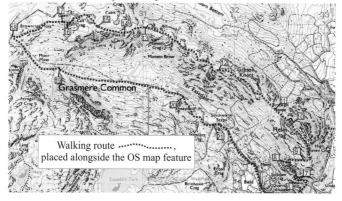

Walking route ················,
placed alongside the OS map feature

The GPS Waypoint lists provided in this book are as recorded by Charles Davis while researching the detailed walk descriptions. Waypoint symbols are numbered so that they can be directly identified with the walk description and waypoint list. All GPS Waypoints are subject to the accuracy of GPS units in the particular location of each waypoint.

In the dramatic landscapes of the Lake District, GPS reception is surprisingly good for the majority of Charles' walking routes.

Satellite Reception

Accurate location fixes for your GPS unit depend upon you receiving signals from four or more satellites. Providing you have good batteries, and that you wait until your GPS has full 'satellite acquisition' before starting out, your GPS will perform well in the Lake District. Where Charles has encountered poor satellite reception it is mentioned in the walk description.

Manually Inputting Waypoints

GPS Waypoints are quoted for the OSGB (Ordnance Survey Great Britain) datum and BNG (British National Grid) coordinates, making them identical with the OS grid coordinates of the position they refer to. To manually input the Waypoints into your GPS we suggest that you:

- switch on your GPS and select 'simulator/standby' mode
- check that your GPS is set to the OSGB datum and BNG 'location/position format'
- input the GPS Waypoints into a 'route' with the same number as the walking route; then when you call up the 'route' in the Lake District there will be no confusion as to which walking route it refers
- repeat the inputting of waypoints into routes until you have covered all the routes you plan to walk, or until you have used up the memory capacity of your GPS
- turn off your GPS. When you turn your GPS back on it should return to its normal navigation mode.

Note that GPS Waypoints complement the routes in Walk! The Lake District South, and are not intended as an alternative to the detailed walking route descriptions.

Personal Navigator Files (PNFs) CD version 3.01

Edited versions of Charles Davis' original GPS research tracks and waypoints are available as downloadable files on our PNFs CD, which also includes all the edited GPS tracks and waypoints for all the Walk!/Walks guide books published by DWG along with GPS Utility Special Edition software. See DWG websites for more information

www.walking.demon.co.uk & www.dwgwalking.co.uk

GPS The Easy Way (£4.99)

If you are confused by talk of GPS, but are interested in how this modern navigational aid could enhance your walking enjoyment, then simply seek out a copy of GPS The Easy Way, the UK's best selling GPS manual.

ESKDALE (The Walks, pages 25-38)

Eskdale from Harter Fell

Eskdale has been a natural way into the **Lake District** since Roman times, when it was the main route from the port of **Glannoventa** (modern **Ravenglass**) to **Ambleside**, so it seemed appropriate that we use it as our own gateway. The wool trade and mining acted as a bridge between the days when it was a military supply line and its contemporary role as a tourist destination, and both intermediary industries have left traces that nowadays feature as visitor attractions.

The main settlements, **Ravenglass**, **Eskdale Green** and **Boot**, are linked by a narrow gauge railway, **La'al Ratty**, which was built for transporting granite and ore, and now provides a pleasant alternative to the full loop of Walk 4. This section also includes two walks to the south of **Eskdale** in the fells behind **Millom**. Though geographically distinct, these itineraries are well placed as first walks en route to **Eskdale**, or for a farewell outing on the day of departure. **Sunkenkirk** is a well preserved stone circle, an easy stroll from the main road, while the slightly more strenuous ascent of **Black Combe** takes us onto a summit that, weather permitting, is said to enjoy one of the most extensive panoramas in Britain, celebrated in Wordsworth's 'View from the Top of Black Combe'.

See Appendices for accommodation information.

WASDALE (The Walks, pages 39-60)

This is the place of superlatives, in part because, as every guidebook will tell you, it boasts England's highest summit, deepest lake, smallest church, and biggest liar (Will Ritson, a nineteenth century publican, given to telling tales as tall as the surrounding mountains), but in the main because it inspires otherwise sober individuals to start babbling about the glories of nature, as if the Romantics had not already elevated such sentiments to orthodoxy. I'll resist that temptation, but you can understand why many succumb.

Wasdale from Great Gable

This is the wild end of the southern **Lake District**, boasting a landscape of quite exceptional drama.

The mountains are just that little bit grander and little bit wilder than elsewhere (it's no accident that **Wasdale** is considered the home of English rock climbing), and better still there's none of the elaborate tourist infrastructure that can give the lie to what remains of the wilderness in other areas. Just the pub, the car park, and a couple of campsites. Suffice to say that, for all the fabulous views available in the **Lake District**, **Great Gable** seen from **Wast Water** is the emblem of the National Park.

There are no refreshments to be had on any of the walks, but **Strands Hotel** in **Nether Wasdale** deserves a mention for great beer and good food. The only drawback, they aren't generally open until the evening. The **Wasdale Head Inn** was temporarily closed due to fire when we were researching the area, but enjoys a good reputation.

See Appendices for accommodation information.

DUNNERDALE (The Walks, pages 61-68)

No lake and not much in the way of its own mountains, but **Dunnerdale**, or the **Duddon Valley**, is such a sublime spot Wordsworth dedicated an entire book to it (The Duddon Sonnets, 1820), reckoning it one of the finest valleys in the region. For online text of the sonnets, see www.bartleby.com.

Dunnerdale from the Coniston Fells

Seathwaite (not to be confused with the **Seathwaite** in **Borrowdale**) was also the home of "Wonderful Walker", who is immortalized in one of the Duddon Sonnets and further commemorated by an inscribed stone outside the local church. "Wonderful Walker" was not, so far as I know, an unusually gifted pedestrian, but Robert Walker, parson of the church for 67 years in the eighteenth century and deemed 'wonderful' for his charity.

Despite the region's general popularity, **Dunnerdale** still has a remote, almost abandoned feel to it, as if the rush to fill the rest of the Lake District with holiday lets and tailored paths has somehow passed the place by. This is not to say that it doesn't get crowded. But go on a weekday out of season and there's every chance you'll have the valley to yourself.

See Appendices for accommodation information.

GREAT LANGDALE (The Walks, pages 69-82)

Stickle Tarn from Harrison Stickle

Although the **Langdale** valley didn't get electricity till the 1960s, its central location, relative ease of access, and outstanding crags, have ensured it has been one of the most popular Lakeland walking areas for generations. It also has the added distinction, surely unique amid holiday destinations, of having been the site of a thriving arms trade. The green rock found below **Pike o' Stickle** was worked by Neolithic man into ax and spear heads, which were subsequently polished on the coast then exported throughout what would become the Celtic fringe. Some of the scree is the spoil of this trade.

Most people will want to be on the spot for the start of the main walks and will probably choose to stay at the **Dungeon Ghyll** inns or **Great Langdale** campsite. However, we have also included two itineraries that can be started from the **Baysbrown Campsite** at **Chapel Stile**, which is further down the road and, at the time of writing, very cheap. The area is also within striking distance of **Ambleside** and **Coniston**.

See Appendices for accommodation information.

CONISTON (The Walks, pages 83-98)

Arthur Ransome, Jeremy Fisher, Jemima Puddleduck, John Ruskin...

No prizes for guessing the odd one out and yet the association is not forced. Ruskin, the foremost art critic of the nineteenth century, lived on the shores of **Coniston Water**, one of the lakes that inspired 'Swallows and Amazons', barely a mile away from Beatrix Potter's future home and the places featured in many of her most famous stories.

Coniston from The Old Man

In terms of walking, **Coniston** is no less celebrated, though there remains an element of paradox. Generations of children have been turned off walking for life after being dragged up the **Old Man of Coniston** by their parents during summer holidays, yet this panjandrum remains a magnet for dedicated walkers and holidaymakers alike. A lively local community and a full range of facilities to fit most tastes and pockets make **Coniston** an excellent base.

The other inestimable advantage the town enjoys is the Coniston Brewing Company. A pint of Bluebird at the **Black Bull Inn** is essential drinking.

And where, you may ask, is the Old Man? Scanning the list of walks in this section, you may have noticed the most famous itinerary in the **Lake District** is missing. In fact, it features in the **Dunnerdale** section, since to my mind this is a more interesting approach, and there seemed little purpose detailing an itinerary so classic it's become a cliché.

See Appendices for accommodation information.

GRASMERE (The Walks, pages 99-107)

"The loveliest spot that man hath ever found", that was Wordsworth's verdict on Grasmere and it's here that the most famous of his Lakeland homes are located. Perhaps inevitably the popularity of the place and attempts to preserve its charms have resulted in something of a museum piece, but **Grasmere's** location is as fabulous as ever, and it remains a useful springboard for exploring the mountains.

The old **Easedale Road** car park has been built on, so anyone arriving by car must park in one of the central car parks. All walks start on the same permissive path. In the unlikely event of this being closed, start on the 'Easedale Road' in front of **Sam Read's Bookshop**, 75 metres from **The Red Lion**.

See Appendices for accommodation information.

AMBLESIDE (The Walks, pages 108-115)

Dickens, when he came to visit the heart of Wordsworth country, was a bit sniffy about **Ambleside**. Sandwich papers, discarded porter bottles, raucous ferry whistles, brass bands, charabancs, uncommonly bibulous locals, and more touts than a day at the races, all feature in a description that betrays an author not always at ease with vulgar good fun. Some claim little has changed. To be honest, it seems a fairly sedate sort of place to me, its chief distinction being a phenomenal number of budget outdoors shops and even more phenomenal number of B&Bs.

Whatever your opinion though, there is one undeniable fact: Ambleside's location is as strategic today as it was in Roman times when it was an important waystage between the coast and the hinterland, and if you want one central base from where you can branch out all over the southern Lake District during a longer holiday, this is probably it.

For a traditional 'pint and pie' pub as opposed to a wannabe restaurant, **The Golden Rule** at the foot of the **Kirkstone Road** is highly recommended. If you're looking to treat yourself to a picnic that's a little superior to the average ham sandwich, **Lucy's Deli** on **Church Street** is such a cornucopia, the chances are you won't be able to get your rucksack off the floor after you've filled it with everything that tempts you.

TROUTBECK (The Walks, pages 116-120)

Troutbeck is an attractive little hamlet stretching along a slip road overlooking the A592 and has been a Conservation Area since 1981. Apart from its setting amid a lovely pastoral landscape, the village has three claims to fame: **Townend**, a yeoman's house now owned by the National Trust and home to a fascinating collection of domestic artifacts; **Troutbeck Park Farm**, Beatrix Potter's sheep farm; and the east window of the local church, which was designed by Burne Jones, William Morris and Ford Maddox Brown.

Walking the ridge (Walk 30)

Given the limited public transport, we only feature two itineraries here, but as everywhere in the Lake District, there are dozens of signposted paths and it would be relatively easy to extend a weekend break by piecing together your own itineraries or filching a few from neighbouring areas, notably **Ambleside** and **Kentmere**.

See Appendices for accommodation information.

KENDAL & KENTMERE (The Walks, pages 117-130)

Direct trains, regular express coaches, plentiful accommodation, a local economy not wholly dependent on tourism, and a host of minor roads forking into the mountains, make **Kendal** a perfect gateway to the southern Lake District. The walks in the immediate vicinity of the town are not among the major, 'must do' itineraries, but they're none the worse for that, and ease of access makes the town ideal for a quick countryside break.

Kentmere lies to the north of **Kendal** and has had the good sense to arrange to be an end of the road community. As is so often the case with topography, 'the end of the road' is an altogether more positive epithet than in common parlance, meaning no through traffic, remote countryside, and a welcome dearth of conventional tourism.

See Appendices for accommodation information.

HAWESWATER (The Walks, pages 131-138)

Frank Westcott (Author of **Walk! The Peak District (South)**) tells how his father descended from **Long Stile** late one evening in the 1930s, navigating with an out of date map and looking forward to a quiet pint in the pub at **Mardale Green**, only to discover that Manchester City Fathers had seen fit to plant a socking great reservoir in the valley, swallowing **Mardale**, pub and all!

Wescott Senior's frustration has been transmuted into our satisfaction for the resulting reservoir is one of the loveliest stretches of water in the Lake District, made all the better by being another 'end of the road' destination, with nothing to attract anyone but the views, the walking, and the wildlife, all of which are fabulous. Birdwatchers will already be familiar with the place, as it is here that, until recently, the last pair of Golden Eagles in England had their nest.

See Appendices for accommodation information.

Haweswater from Harter Fell

1 SUNKENKIRK: SWINSIDE STONE CIRCLE

Throughout the book we feature a number of low level walks for those days when the sky gives up its struggle against gravity and subsides groundwards to get matey with your ankles. The first of these walks is ultralow level and should be accessible in all weathers. **Swinside Stone Circle** or **Sunkenkirk** is one of the best preserved Neolithic monuments in the Lake District, second only to **Castelrigg** which inspired Keats' gloomy musings in Hyperion. In this instance, 'second best' is something of an encomium, as this quietly evocative spot is seldom visited, despite being very easy to reach, and is considerably more engaging than Keats' 'dismal cirque'. The name 'sunkenkirk' stems from a legend that a church or kirk was erected on the spot and promptly swallowed into the underworld by a disgruntled devil, who didn't care for Christian edifices cluttering up pagan places of worship.

The walking is easy and there are no objective obstacles en route, though that may depend on how objective you find the bull that features in two separate warning signs. Said 'bull' was apparently passing himself off as an uncommonly timid sheep the day we researched this walk, but some discretion may be required if the beast is about and behaving in a violently objective manner.

| 1 | 2 H | 5 miles/8km | ︿︿ | 180m 180m | ↻ | 0* |

*The nearest refreshments are in **Broughton** or **Millom**.

Access: by car or bus (from **Broughton** or **Millom**)

> **Stroll**
> **Sunkenkirk** from Wp.8

We start in the village of **Hallthwaites**, which lies on the A595 immediately North of the eastern junction with the A5093 to **Millom**, setting off either from the bus stop/layby directly behind the church, or from the large lay-by in front of **Thwaites School** (Wp.1 0M). From the school, we walk down the village road towards **Duddon Sands** then turn left immediately before the junction with the **Lady Hall** road, and take a footpath signposted 'Thwaites Mill' (Wp.2 6M).

We follow the footpath alongside **Black Beck**, then cross a field and go through a gate onto a lovely path running along the edge of **Fox's Wood** (Wp.3 12M). At the northern limit of the wood, we cross a stile emblazoned with a 'Beware of the bull' sign and two right of way arrows (Wp.4 15M). Bearing right (NE), we cross the bull's field, off-path, skirting a satellite wood at the far end of which there's a stone stile (Wp.5 22M). Walking alongside a wall, we continue off-path into the next field (Wp.6), where a

On the path to Fox's Wood

fence on our left serves as a guiding line onto a rough track, which leads into the **Cornal Ground** farmyard. We then follow the farm's roughly metalled access track up to the A595 and cross onto the 'Broadgate' lane (Wp.7 35M).

100 yards along the lane, we turn right on **Beck Bank Farm** track (Wp.8) then bear left behind the farm (Wp.9) to ford **Black Beck** via partially submerged stepping stones (N.B. If you don't want to risk getting your feet wet, continue along **Broadgate Lane** then turn right to rejoin the

described route at Wp.10).
After the beck, we cross two fields, north across the first, west across the second, to a pair of semi-detached houses distinguished from one another by yellow and blue trim window sills. Going through a gap in the wall immediately behind the houses, we turn right on a lane climbing towards **Thwaites Fell** (Wp.10 45M).

Crossing Black Beck Ford

Swinside Stone Circle

We stroll along the lane in the lee of the small but distinctive fell of **Knott Hill**, then fork left on the **Swinside Farm** bridleway track for 'Swinside Stone Circle'/'Thwaites Fell' (Wp.11 50M). We now simply follow this partially metalled track, initially climbing steadily then virtually on the level, until we reach the stone circle, which is to the right of the track (Wp.12 65M).

Our return route lies to the west of **Knott Hill**. Retracing our steps to the last gateway across the track just short of the stone circle, we cut across **Knott Moor** (S) aiming slightly to the right of **Knott Hill** to join the very faint traces of an ancient trail (more readily discernible from a distance than on the ground) leading to a kissing gate and yet another 'Beware of the bull' sign (Wp.13 79M). Maintaining a southerly direction on a faint but easily followed path, we cross a rough track 50 yards from the gate, then go over a stile, beyond which the path becomes a broad grassy track. After going through another gate (Wp.14 83M), the track disappears in a long, rough, sweeping pasture.

The right of way descends diagonally across this pasture to Wp.17, but is so marshy, we stay on the high ground, following intermittent cow paths and tractor tracks alongside the wall on our left. We then go through a gateless gateway in the southeastern corner of the pasture (Wp.15 91M) and immediately turn right through a breach in a wall to descend on a cow path to the end of a rough track (Wp.16). Bearing right, we curve across a small field to join a major, well-stabilized track (Wp.17 94M).

Doubling back to the left, we follow this track until it veers left across open pasture, at which point we maintain our southerly direction on a grassy, waymarked trail following the wall on our right. The waymarks guide us across a stile beside a gate, after which we follow the wall on our right through a dogleg and two gateways until we reach the **Bank House** access track (Wp.18 109M). Turning left, we follow the track to the A595 then descend along the road back to our starting point.

2 BLACK COMBE

Black Combe is the solitary, outstanding fell in the Southwestern corner of the National Park and as such is in the vanguard when it comes to the Lake District's confrontation with the elements. Branwell Brontë said **Black Combe** was "formed to fight a thousand years of struggles with a storm" and that it "rejoiced" in stormy skies, Wordsworth spoke of "total gloom" on "the blinded mountain's silent top", and local poet, Norman Nicholson, wryly observed that if you could see **Black Combe** it was going to rain, and if you couldn't, it already was!

But don't let that put you off. It's a lovely, airy little summit reached by a broad, clear trail, easily ascended even amid "far travelled storms of land and sea" (Wordsworth again) and, when the views are available, they're quite splendid. The last stretch after **Townend** is a little dull, but the descent toward **Far End** amply compensates, and the delightful bridleway between **Butcher's Breast** and **Whitbeck** is constantly stimulating. *Combe* in this instance derives not from *cumba*, meaning 'valley', but *camb*, or 'crest'. The first mile is steep, but after that it's easy walking all the way.

3	3½ H	8.7 miles/14 km		600m / 600m	↻	2

Access: by car, train or (Sunday service **Barrow** to **Whitehaven**) bus

Short Version:
linear ascent of **Black Combe**

The walk starts beside **Whicham** Church on the eastbound branch of the A595(T), 450 yards from the junction with the A5093. There's parking in a small lay-by and at the end of the church access lane in front of **Whicham Old School**.

To reach the start from **Silecroft** station, walk up to the A5093 and take the signed right of way across the field slightly to your left, joining the A595 250 yards west of **St. Mary's Church**.

From the car park beside the church (Wp.1 0M), we take the path between the church and the old school, turning left almost immediately on a narrow tarmac lane. When the tarmac ends 350 yards later at **Kirkbank** farm, we continue on the dirt track behind the house for 100 yards then bear right to cross a wooden stile (Wp.2 8M).

The initial climb

Following a broad grassy trail traversing close-cropped sward and a patchwork of wind battered bracken, we climb steadily toward the smoothly sculpted head of **Moorgill Beck**. After crossing a narrow dirt track (Wp.3 18M), we continue our steady climb along the watercourse until the gradient eases at a marshy pass (Wp.4 34M) above the swale at the head of the beck, from where the western shoulder (not the summit!) of **Black Combe** is visible.

After a long gentle northerly climb amid sheets of blackened broom (Wp.5 58M), **Sellafield** comes into view, and the trail levels off for a few hundred yards. A final brief climb brings us to a junction (Wp.6 70M) marked by a large stone arrow and a pile of stones resembling a collapsed pterodactyl, 150 yards below the trig point and windbreak on the flat summit of **Black Combe** (Wp.7 71M).

From the trig point, we head north to rejoin the trail we left at Wp.6 (Wp.8 74M), which we follow down to the left across the

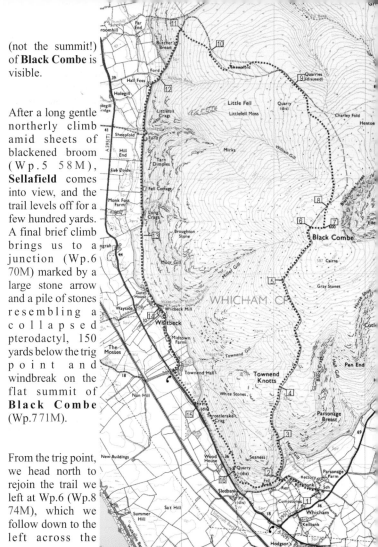

The start of the descent

sweeping moorland behind **William Gill**. After a long gentle descent (N), we reach a level stretch overlooking a final plateau on the edge of the fell (Wp.9 94M). The trail gradually curves west, passing a ruined sheepfold hemmed in by clumps of marsh grass, 300 yards after which we fork left at a Y-junction (Wp.10 109M), and descend to a gate in a fence (Wp.11 115M).

The Hall Foss ruin

Staying on the nearside of the fence, we turn left and follow it (SW) down toward a ruin, shortly before which, we cross **Halfloss Beck** (Wp.12 125M). Continuing (S) alongside the wall that has replaced the fence, we cross **Holegill Beck** and pass the abandoned **Fell Cottage**, where the trail is waterlogged and patched, somewhat precariously, with rotten planks peeled from the cottage fence.

After a second muddy patch, we fork left at a Y-junction (Wp.13 151M), maintaining altitude before rejoining the main wall-side trail 400 yards later, shortly before it runs into a roughly stabilized lane in front of the gates of **Whitbeck Mill** (Wp.14 162M).

At the end of the lane, we join the A595, which we follow (S) on a wide verge for 200 yards until we reach a signposted path climbing to the left (Wp.15 176M), where we have a choice of routes. The simplest way to return to our starting point (not recommended!) is to follow the road for another 900 yards until a clear path climbs to the left, leading into the track back to **Kirkbank** farm.

To minimise the road walking though, I suggest turning left at the signpost and climbing steeply for 100 yards until the **Black Combe** path goes through a metal gate. Immediately after the gate, we turn right and follow the fence as it runs parallel to the road, ignoring clearer sheep-walks climbing to the left. Our 'path' is very narrow and maybe overgrown in Summer, in which case you'll have to pick your way along the fence as best you can or resort to the road. Eventually, we come to a locked metal gate below an old quarry (Wp.16 189M). If the inside of the fence is overgrown, climb over the gate to join the **Kirkbank** track. Otherwise, we continue inside the fence, climbing to skirt a couple of clumps of thorny brush before rejoining our outward route at Wp.2 (201M).

Not one for your peak-baggers, nor for those with a strong antipathy to damp socks (in places the turf gets so soggy you begin to wish somebody's god would dig it up and give it a good wringing), but if you like roaming over wild wet moorland with fine views of high mountains, this itinerary is a good first walk, and a useful option when the summits are under cloud. If you're arriving by car, park at **Dalegarth** Station.

1 | 2¾ H | 6.3 miles/9½km | 200m / 200m | ↻ | 4*

* at the **Boot** Inn

Access: on foot from **Boot**

The walk starts at the northern end of the lane into **Boot**, on the nearside of the **Eskdale Mill** bridge (Wp.1 0M). We take the signposted bridleway/footpath on the right for 'Eel Tarn', climbing alongside the cascading waters of **Whillan Beck**. Ignoring a footpath to the right after 75 yards and a track forking right after 175 yards, we stay on the roughly asphalted bridleway until the tarmac ends (Wp.2 8M), at which point we turn right, going through a gate to join the signposted 'Eel Tarn' path.

The path runs alongside a wall for 300 yards before reaching a divergence of ways (Wp.3 13M). Ignoring the branch going through a gate on the right, we maintain direction (NE) between two walls, bringing into view the great rise of **Sca Fell** massif. When the wall on the left curves west, we continue alongside the wall on the right into a subtly mottled palette of pale greens, soft browns and gun-metal grey. The right hand wall soon bears away from our path, too, and we continue (ENE) on a rocky, waterlogged trail. After crossing a grassy rise overlooking the broad bowl of affluent springs feeding **Whillan Beck**, we pick our way across marshy ground to a confluence of ways (Wp.4 28M), 200 yards north of **Eel Tarn**; invisible from this point.

Bearing left, we follow a green trail snaking through banks of brown bracken, the dry grassy rises interspersed by patches of marsh dappled with ore rich rocks. After we've passed between a sheepfold and a large outcrop of rock with a faint white cross daubed on its southern face (Wp.5 40M), **Hardrigg** and **Oliver Gills** come into view at the head of **Whillan Beck**, and our path

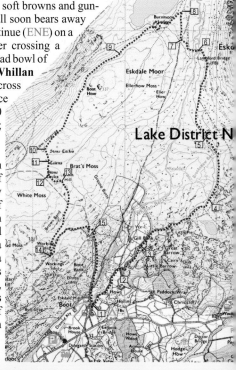

Lambford Bridge

curves down to **Lambford Bridge** (Wp.6 57M). Crossing the bridge, we climb away from the beck for 50 yards then curve northwest to join the cairn-marked **Corpse Road** (Wp.7 62M) linking **Wasdale** with **Eskdale** cemetery. We follow the **Corpse Road** north for 250 yards until we come to an inverted Y-junction (Wp.8

Burnmoor Lodge

67M), from where we see **Burnmoor Tarn** for the first time. Doubling back to the left, we pass directly behind the squat, square cottage of **Burnmoor Lodge** (a pleasant spot for a picnic if the ground's dry) and follow the higher of two narrow sheep walks as it bears away from the southern

Miterdale

end of the tarn. The path curves WSW round a high shoulder and crosses a dry watershed (Wp.9 93M) facing the falls at **Miterdale Head**, after which it becomes fainter and grassier, but still easy to follow as it's the only natural way along the contour. Fine views open out to the south, first of **Muncaster Fell** and **Ravenglass** sands, then of lower **Miterdale**, as our path edges onto relatively level terrain above **Low Longrigg**.

At a Y-junction (Wp.10 112M), we fork left, passing what appears to be a small barrow before reaching a row of stones stacked on a large rock (Wp.11). The path becomes obscure for 50 yards, but maintaining a southerly direction for 125 yards, we join a clear trail between **White** and **Brat's Mosses** (Wp.12 117M). Turning left, we come to a circle of standing stones (Wp.13 119M), where we bear right, following a broad trail to the right of a second, less distinct stone circle, after which **Eel Tarn** is visible on the far side of the valley.

Staying with the main trail (S) we cross a couple of small rises within sight of the ruined peat huts above **Boot**. Joining a broader, cairn-marked trail (Wp.14 133M), we double back to the left and descend past a fenced mineshaft, initially parallel to the path from the stone circles, then gradually curving east to descend to the peat huts, two of which are still roofed. The way becomes obscure again, but between the two roofed huts (Wp.15 149M) we recover a clear stony trail descending (S) alongside a wall, eventually going through a gate to enter **Boot** via the **Eskdale Mill** bridge.

4 A RIVER ESK ROUND

Apart from a few boggy bits and one stretch where pathfinding is difficult, this is an easy low level walk across varied terrain, incorporating a famous waterfall, a remote lake, a riverside stroll, and a small fell with views way above its station. The high exertion rating is due to length and I suspect most people will want to break the itinerary in two, returning in each case via the **La'al Ratty** narrow gauge railway. If you have a preference for the beaten path, you should opt for Short Version (b), as the descent from **Devoke Water** to the **River Esk** is complicated by boggy ground and an invisible right-of-way. The walk starts at one of our suggested accommodation options, the **Fisherground Farm** campsite; which has its own stop on the **La'al Ratty** line, but can easily be adapted to start from **Ravenglass Station** (for those arriving by car or train) or **Eskdale Green** (using the **Ulpha** road to reach **Forge Bridge** - Wp.46). NOTE: The described approach to **Ravenglass** along the **River Esk** estuary might be submerged by exceptionally high tides. An alternative route is noted in the text, but if you wish to check the tide tables beforehand, call Whitehaven Tourist Information Office on 0845 0952132.

5 | 7.5 H | 19 miles/30 km | 600m / 600m | 3

Access: on foot (various starting points possible)

Strolls

(a) **Stanley Force** (b) **Devoke Water** (from Wp.14 - adequate roadside parking) (c) **Muncaster Woods** (Wps.29-26)

Short Versions

(a) **Eskdale** to **Ravenglass** returning by La'al Ratty narrow gauge railway
(b) **Ravenglass** to **Eskdale** returning by La'al Ratty narrow gauge railway
(c) **Muncaster Fell** from **Muncaster Gardens** car-park

From the campsite entrance (Wp.1 0M), we take the footpath to 'Milkingstead Bridge', where we cross the **River Esk** and turn left. Following a bridleway track along the left bank of the **Esk**, we go through a gated field cutting a bend in the river (Wp.2 6M). After briefly narrowing to a path, the bridleway widens again and passes a branch climbing to the right (Wp.3 16M).

At a second junction (Wp.4 27M), we fork left then bear right to pass behind **Dalegarth Hall**, unmistakable with its five, stout round chimneys. After 200 yards, we leave the bridleway, turning right for 'Stanley Gill / Birker Fell' (Wp.5 33M) and going through a gate 75 yards later as directed by a 'Waterfalls' sign (Wp.6).

Following a clear path, we climb gently alongside the gill amid mossy rocks and spindly limbed oaks.

Dalegarth Hall

Ignoring a minor fork to the right (Wp.7 41M), we cross three footbridges, passing a second turning between the last two bridges (GPS reception is poor here) just short of **Stanley Force**. Having viewed the waterfall, we retrace our steps and take the path climbing from between the second and third bridges, following an affluent to a junction of paths at a tiny two-slab footbridge (Wp.8 52M).

Turning left, we climb to a rock-platform viewing-point just below a wooden stile (Wp.9 57M). The platform is vertiginous, but does not have to be crossed to continue the walk, hence the absence of a vertigo warning. The drop can better be appreciated by crossing the stile and following the fence down to the left, where a wooden bridge and narrow path lead to a second viewing point (not counted in subsequent timings).

Sca Fell in the background

For the main walk, once across the stile, we head south for 75 yards to join a dirt track. Bearing left, we follow the track to the SE, fine views opening out behind us of **Sca Fell** and the surrounding high summits. After passing a small stand of pine, the track goes through a gate beside the **Low Ground** farmhouse (Wp.10 68M).

From here it is possible to fork right and climb directly across the moor to **Birker Fell**, but since this involves scaling two fences clearly not designed for scaling, I can't really recommend it!

Instead, we cross the stile beside the farmhouse and follow the track down to a stand of pine (Wp.11 70M).

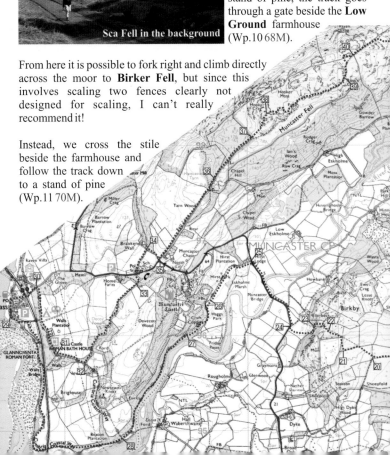

The white house at the other end of the track is **High Ground** farm, situated just below Wp.13. Unfortunately, the track's not a right-of-way and goes through a working farmyard, so we have to trace a dogleg via **Birkerthwaite Farm**.

Forking left on the wayposted footpath, we pass to the left of the pine and cross a stone bridge into a field. Following a faint track, we traverse interlinked pastures, going through two gates, after which the track becomes clearer, climbing to cross the yard behind **Ganny Cottage** and join the main access track (Wp.12 80M). Bearing right, we follow this track to a signposted junction above **High Ground** farmhouse (Wp.13 88M), where we turn left to reach the **Ulpha** road (Wp.14 93M).

Crossing the road, we stroll along a bridleway track to **Devoke Water**, where there's a boathouse backed by a ruin. 45 yards before the track reaches the boathouse, we turn left (Wp.15 110M) on a rough trodden way curving round the southern side of the lake. Staying as near the water as we can (probably not very near given the marshy ground), we follow a series of faint parallel ways shadowing the shoreline, aiming to join a broad grassy trail at the western end of the lake beside a knee-high cairn (Wp.16 133M).

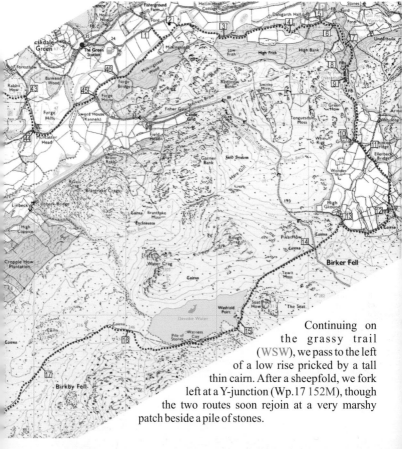

Continuing on the grassy trail (WSW), we pass to the left of a low rise pricked by a tall thin cairn. After a sheepfold, we fork left at a Y-junction (Wp.17 152M), though the two routes soon rejoin at a very marshy patch beside a pile of stones.

The stubby silhouette of **Stainton Tower** serves as our next objective, though our real goal is **Muncaster Castle**, first seen from a second Y-junction (Wp.18 164M). Forking right, we pass what looks like an old dewpond but features on the map as 'Barnscar settlement', after which we descend to a wayposted route going through a gate in a wall beside a sheepfold (Wp.19 172M). After the gate, a clear, but occasionally boggy trail leads to the top of the next field, where the wayposted route swings left alongside a wall (Wp.20 181M).

We leave the wayposted route here and climb over a rusty metal gate. N.B. The route we follow for the next few hundred yards does not coincide exactly with the right-of-way marked on the OS map, but is the most practical on the ground.

Climbing (NW) on a narrow path, we pass between two small outcrops of rock on the brow of the hill and continue onto a second rise, bringing **Muncaster Castle** back into view. The path disappears here. Ignoring a sheep walk descending into the next field, we stay on the nearside of the wall and head west, bringing **Stainton Tower** back into view. Immediately after a T formed by a wall descending to our right, we cross steps set in the wall (Wp.21 187M).

Our next objective is a stile on the lower edge of the next field, just to the right of the wood on **Ellerbeck Crag**. Unfortunately, this field is very boggy, so we bear right and follow the fence/wall on our right (N), picking our way across tufts of grass and staying away from the marshiest area in the middle of the field.

After crossing a tumbledown lateral wall (incidentally intersecting with the invisible right-of-way), we pass a small stand of trees and follow the wall on our right down to a sturdy new fence. 30 yards to our left is a new stile (Wp.22 195M), which also happens to be out of sync with the OS mapped right-of-way. Once over it we descend alongside the wall on our right (still off-path and still, strictly speaking, not on the right-of-way, but strictly speaking the right-of-way is indescribable) then follow the wall round to the left, where we find another stile (Wp.23 204M) hidden from above by trees. At this point you can relax, as the pathfinding problems are over. We now simply descend directly across an open field to a gate onto the A595 (Wp.24 208M).

We now have the least agreeable stretch of the walk, following the road north for half a mile until we come to a blue-trimmed gatehouse, **Hirst Lodge**, where we turn left into **Muncaster Estate** on a dirt track signposted 'Cumbria Coastal Way' (Wp.25 220M). (NOTE: a variant of the **Cumbria Coastal Way** leaves the road just before **Muncaster Bridge**, but this leads to a ford that's only viable when the tide is at its lowest).

The track curves round marshland below **Muncaster Castle** then climbs into the castle gardens, at which point we bear left on a signposted path (Wp.26 230M) going through a kissing gate. The path crosses a couple of footbridges and winds through storm ravaged woodland carpeted with bluebells, then joins another track into the main estate (Wp.27 239M).

Bearing left, we follow the **River Esk**, passing a signposted ford and a turning on the right (Wp.28 256M) - an alternative way of reaching Wp.32 and

Ravenglass if the main path is too muddy or the tide is high. Mud and tides permitting, we continue along the river, burrowing through more woodland before going under the main railway line (NOTE: if you're doing Stroll (c), this is the third railway bridge along the estuary) and emerging in the estuary.

There's no path as such here, simply an intermittently trodden way across the grassy flats along the fringe of the estuary, passing two more railway bridges, the second of which frames an alternative access to Wp.31.

'Roman bath house'

After this last bridge, the estuary way becomes less grassy and follows hard packed shingle and mud flats. We can stay on the flats all the way to **Ravenglass** or take an embankment path 250 yards after the last railway bridge. Either way, we enter the village via the main route in front of **Esk View House** (Wp.29 296M).

For the pub, tea garden, car-park and trains, we stroll along the main street then turn right just before the post-office. The **La'al Ratty** station is on the far side of the mainline station and is accessible via a footbridge. The last train is at 4.30 p.m. By this stage, taking the train may seem the only sane option.

Otherwise, having refreshed ourselves in the facilities round the stations, we take the path that is a continuation of the railway footbridge, passing between a playground and children's football field. Turning right at a T-junction with a tarmac lane (Wp.30 301M), we pass the **Ravenglass** campsite entrance and follow a cinder path alongside a private road. After passing the ruins of the Roman bath house, we branch left at a Y-junction of tracks (Wp.31) then turn left in front of two large houses (Wp.32 315M), both turnings bearing blue signs for 'Muncaster'.

The track climbs through pleasant woodland, passing a small dam, after which we fork right at a Y-junction (Wp.33 327M) to pass the entrance to **Muncaster Gardens**. Following the driveway down to the A595, we take the bridleway out of the car-park on the far side of the road, then turn right at the crossroads below **Branken Wall Farm** (Wp.34 332M) to return to the road. Rejoining the road 250 yards from the castle entrance, we turn left on **Fell Lane** for 'Muncaster Fell' (Wp.35 335M).

After a long gentle climb, **Fell Lane** dips into **Tarn Wood**, where we come to a signposted junction (Wp.36 348M).

Muncaster Fell

Continuing straight ahead for 'Eskdale', we pass **Muncaster Tarn** (a pleasant place marred by moribund pine), after which we go through a kissing-gate within sight of the trig point on the fell's highest summit, **Hooker Crag**. Forking left at the end of the woods (Wp.37 357M), we leave the main trail and follow a clear path climbing onto **Hooker Crag** (Wp.38 362M), from where we have fine views of the park's major peaks.

After descending directly to the east, we bear southeast to rejoin the main trail skirting **Hooker Moss**. We then pass an inscribed dolmen dated 1886 (Wp.39 378M) and veer north to circumvent more marshy land before going through a gateway in a wall within sight of **Eskdale Green** (Wp.40 385M). Picking our way across rough, intermittently waterlogged ground, we descend toward **Silver Knott**, the final rise of the fell, either following the official right-of-way or the drier more southerly route beaten out by walkers. We cross the **Silver Knott** ridge at the obvious pass on its southern side, where the path is flanked by two standing stones (Wp.41 399M).

Ignoring a couple of sheep walks climbing to the left, we descend steadily to a kissing gate (Wp.42 408M). The trail then traverses attractive scrubland down to a confluence of ways at a stile (Wp.43 414M). For **Irton Road Station**, turn left. For the pub and **Eskdale Green**, take the signposted bridleway across the field in front of you. For **Fisherground** campsite, we turn right and follow the track down to **Muncaster Head Farm**. Passing to the right of the cow sheds, we turn left in front of the farm (Wp.44 420M) and take the access track to the **Ulpha** road (Wp.45 429M). Turning left on the **Ulpha** road then right on the track at **Forge Bridge** (Wp.46 433M), we return to **Milkingstead Bridge** and our starting point.

What to do on a wet day in **Wasdale** apart from whiling away the time in the pub? It's a question you'll probably have to ask yourself at some stage during your visit and hopefully this itinerary will provide an answer, at least in part. Even when comparatively low hills like **Illgill Head** are swathed in mist, visibility on **Middle Fell** is generally reasonable, and the climb along **Greendale Gill** is a pleasant excursion in its own right, feeling far more remote than it's physical proximity to tarmac would suggest.

This is also a good outing for a first day to get a feel for the area. In late spring/early summer, there's a particularly fine display of foxgloves amid the bracken at the beginning of the walk.

Access by car:
We start from **Greendale** hamlet, 600 yards west of the junction between the **Nether Wasdale** and **Gosforth** roads. There's plenty of free parking on the large grassy area immediately east of the hamlet on the northern side of the road.

From Wp.1

From the parking area (Wp.1 0M), we take the broad grassy trail cutting through the bracken to the north, climbing steadily to traverse a level knoll, from where we already have an attractive view on **Wast Water**. Still climbing steadily, we pass the grassy path descending off **Middle Fell** (Wp.2 13M) and continue up the valley, now virtually on the level, for another 250 yards, following a narrow, rugged path.

When the path reaches **Greendale Gill** (Wp.3 17M), we can either continue along the gill's left bank (our right) or, as mapped, ford the gill for a better view of the **Tongue Gill** water chutes before continuing on the right bank. Taking **Greendale Gill** as our guideline, we follow faint sheep walks shadowing the watercourse.

The sheep walks eventually converge with the gill and peter out, but I recommend staying on the right bank, as it tends to be slightly drier than the main path. In either case, the course of the gill soon levels off amid open moorland for the final slightly marshy approach to **Greendale Tarn** (Wp.4 40M).

Bearing left, we skirt the western side of the tarn, initially on a faint sheep walk, but soon off path as we climb away from the soggier ground around the tarn, aiming for the col between **Seatallan** and **Middle Fell**. A little way below the col, we fork right on a very faint way (Wp.5 52M) climbing to the

outcrops of rock at the base of **Middle Fell**, where we join a reasonably clear path (Wp.6 55M).

Bearing right, we climb gently then steadily (SSE) onto the back of the fell (Wp.7 67M). The faint path meanders along the fell in a southerly direction, passing a large pile of stones marking the highest outcrop of rock (Wp.8 74M).

The subsequent descent follows a generally southwesterly orientation, though we do occasionally veer off course to circumnavigate rising ground. After briefly swinging west (Wp.9 84M), we descend steadily along a shallow depression (SW), rejoining our outward route at Wp.2 (105M), which we follow back to the start.

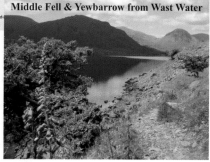

Middle Fell & Yewbarrow from Wast Water

It's now that we go and while away the rest of the day in the pub, either at the **Wasdale Head Inn** or **The Strands** in **Nether Wasdale** (though the latter doesn't open at lunch).

6 ILLGILL HEAD

A classic lowish level loop that boasts a descent with one of the finest views in the **Lake District**, a grand panorama of all the high mountains round **Wasdale** that's perfect for getting the lay of the land or bidding farewell to summits that have become old friends. The return along the shore of **Wast Water** is quite something, too. The flank of **Illgill** is dubbed 'The Screes' and, seen from the western shore, it looks well named. But when you're on them 'the screes' seems a tad euphemistic, since five of the alleged 'screes' are actually rockslides, at least one of which was supplemented by some massive boulders during the Winter of 2005. I've even heard tell of tourists having to be rescued when they got stuck! So long as you're reasonably energetic and like a little rock-hopping, there are no insurmountable obstacles, but the warning notices at either end of the path should not be casually dismissed.

If you're staying at **Wasdale Head**, it's tempting to do the route in reverse, climbing first onto **Illgill Head**. Best resist the temptation, since that would mean swapping superb mountain vistas for a good long look at the **Sellafield** nuclear plant. If transport is lacking, do **The Screes** first then climb onto the ridge.

For a stroll, take the **Easthwaite Farm** driveway/footpath at the start of the walk, then either turn left at Wp.32 to **Lund Bridge** and the permissive path along the shoreline below the **Youth Hostel**, or continue along the described route in reverse until you reach **The Screes**. Alternatively, start from the National Trust car park at **Wasdale Head** and follow the **Wasdale Head Hall Farm** track to join the described route at Wp.21, turning back when you get the impression 'scree' is becoming a faintly surreal understatement.

Access: by car or on foot from **Nether Wasdale**

Stroll Wast Water

We start from the bridge over the **River Irt** at the southern corner of the triangle of slip roads east of **Nether Wasdale**. There's parking for three or four cars in the National Trust lay-by immediately north of the bridge. If these spaces are taken, park in **Nether Wasdale** (there's usually plenty of room in front of the church), and walk to the start.

From the lay-by (Wp.1 0M), we cross the bridge (in the direction of 'Santon Bridge') passing the **Easthwaite Farm** driveway/footpath and turn left immediately after **Flass House** on the bridleway for 'Eskdale' (Wp.2).

Crossing a stile beside **Flass Tarn** (see picture on next page) on the far side of the field (Wp.3 4M), we maintain direction (SE) with a wall on our left, going through another gate 175 yards

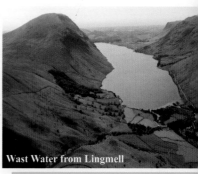

Wast Water from Lingmell

Flass Tarn

later and taking the left fork at a junction with a track 45 yards after that (Wp.4). Continuing alongside the wall as it curves SW we rejoin the track (Wp.5 14M), where we turn left, immediately forking left as indicated to stay on the bridleway. At the next junction (Wp.6 16M), we ignore the 'Wasdale' path on the left and bear right, staying on the 'Eskdale' bridleway. After crossing a narrow canal and overgrown track, we go through a double-gated gateway (Wp.7 19M).

We now follow a rough grassy trail, climbing steeply up **Irton Fell**, initially in a SW direction then weaving back and forth across a broad southerly spectrum as the trail becomes fainter and marshier about midway up the fell. After a couple of large boulders within sight of **Irton Wood** (Wp.8 34M), the gradient eases for the final approach to the woods, 100 yards before which, we fork left (Wp.9 38M).

Almost immediately, we veer sharp left to continue climbing (NNE) on a succession of interlocking grassy trails, passing the corner of the wall that encloses the wood (Wp.10 42M). From hereon in, the upland walking is simply a question of keeping on keeping on, and unless conditions are absolutely foul (which begs the question of what you're doing up here in the first place!), description is largely redundant, so I suggest putting the book away and just enjoying the walk.

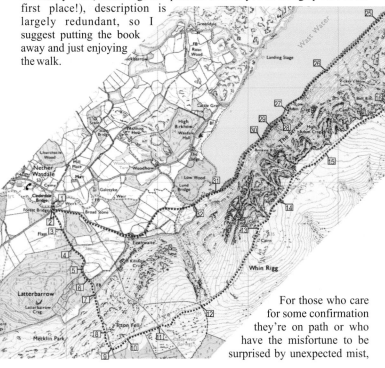

For those who care for some confirmation they're on path or who have the misfortune to be surprised by unexpected mist, we climb gently (NNE) on a clear but occasionally splintered trail to a ladder-stile (Wp.11 47M). Boggy ground briefly obscures the trail immediately after the stile, but climbing in a more easterly direction, we soon recover a clear, unified trail traversing undulating grassland to a tumbledown wall overlooking the green scar of **Greathall Gill**, an alternative but steeper way onto the ridge (Wp.12 57M). From here a straightforward steady climb marked

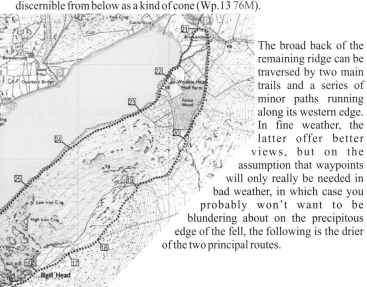

Greathall Gill

with regular, largely redundant cairns, leads to the more northerly **Whin Rigg** summit, a small outcrop of rock blocked in by a tiny windbreak, the whole discernible from below as a kind of cone (Wp.13 76M).

The broad back of the remaining ridge can be traversed by two main trails and a series of minor paths running along its western edge. In fine weather, the latter offer better views, but on the assumption that waypoints will only really be needed in bad weather, in which case you probably won't want to be blundering about on the precipitous edge of the fell, the following is the drier of the two principal routes.

On Illgill Head

Following a clear trail (N), we descend to a Y-junction just short of the two tarns in the central depression of the ridge (Wp.14 81M). We fork left, passing to the left of the tarns, though either branch will do as they rejoin 550 yards later (Wp.15 91M) for the initially steep then increasingly gentle climb to a large cairn on the first of the **Illgill Head** summits (Wp.16 106M), 350 yards from the windbreak on the second summit (Wp.17 111M, see picture on the next page).

250 yards to the northeast, two large cairns mark the start of our glorious descent (Wp.18) on a trail that is always clear and occasionally marked by cairns.

Given the grand panorama of high mountains, the way down passes in a blur of gratifying images, and all too soon, we're

Old Corpse Road

crossing a line of rubble, all that remains of a wall (Wp.19 128M) and the harbinger of the low ground.

Staying on the main trail and ignoring crisscrossing sheep walks, we descend steeply alongside the wall then ford a gill onto an eroded trail feeding into the old **Corpse Road** (Wp.20 141M).

Maintaining direction (NE), we descend past a cluster of evocative little ruins, where the path resumes a more northerly trajectory, going through three gates, the last into the wooded enclosure of **Brackenclose**. There is a shortcut right-of-way down to the lake just before the third gate, but since the gate giving access to it is currently blocked by a large rock and it makes little difference to the overall distance, we go through **Brackenclose**, descending to the bridge over **Lingmell Gill**, where we turn left on the **Wasdale Head Hall Farm** access track (Wp.21 161M).

Crossing a stile just below the farm (Wp.22 170M), we follow a dirt track traversing two enclosed pastures to a gate with a warning notice about **The Screes** path (Wp.23 178M), basically saying it's rough, rocky and slippery. It is, but not yet.

After a gently rising stroll, we see the southern end of the lake and cross a tiny spring (Wp.24 190M), beyond which the path is momentarily obscured by a mishmash of partially interred rocks. The path soon becomes clear again, continuing along a rough contour with a sufficiently steep slope off to the right to make it worthwhile watching exactly where you're putting your feet.

500 yards later we reach the first stretch of scree (Wp.25 199M), where a well trodden way across small, densely packed stones actually makes the walking easier. Not for long, though. Scree of varying degree and size alternates with patches of stony path for the next 350 yards until we traverse a thin band of oak onto a long stretch of scree, the far end of which is slightly loose. The adventure begins! The next stretch of scree (Wp.26 210M) is a rough rock slide, but still easily passed, as are the next three. The fifth is a little more arduous.

a little 'light scree'

Forking left (Wp.27 224M), we climb 20 yards above the lake and begin our painstaking progress across a major rockslide. There's no path, just a lot of big rocks, some of which are still loose, while others have been arranged into a couple of reasonably large cairns (Wp.28 229M) guiding us between the biggest boulders.

'not so light' scree

After going between the boulders, we pass another large cairn (Wp.29 234M) 150 yards from the end of the rockslide and the recovery of a clear path (Wp.30 241M).

After that escapade, the last section of scree is a very self-effacing affair, barely noticed as we make our way to a track beside the **Pump House** at the end of the lake (Wp.31 251M).

200 yards later, we pass a signposted path off to the right (Wp.32), an optional route for those doing the stroll. Otherwise, we simply follow the track back through **Easthwaite Farm** to the start.

A straightforward ascent of the National Park's emblematic peak, but not to be taken lightly. Though relatively short and visiting a solitary summit, this is a major mountain in the context of the **Lake District**, involving an energetic climb, a peak that's no place to be in poor weather, and a steep exposed descent that won't be to everyone's taste. The rewards, though, are commensurate, and on a clear day the views are so good they smack of the sinful. If you have an appetite for the picturesque, gorge yourself and be glad!

| 5 | 3½ H | 5.3 miles/8½ km | 810m / 810m | ↻ | 3 |

Access: on foot from **Wasdale**

> **Stroll**
> **Lingmell Beck**

We start from the large, free parking area toward the end of the **Wasdale Head** road, on the 'Lingmell House B&B'/'Wasdale Head Church' bridleway (Wp.1 0M).

Waypoint 1

Strolling along the track toward the church, we can already see the path climbing across the lower slopes of **Great Gable** to **Sty Head**. Bearing left at **Burnthwaite Farm** (Wp.2 10M), we follow a stony track that ends at a footbridge over **Gable Beck**, immediately after which, we pass our return route from **Beck Head** (Wp.3 22M).

Continuing on a broad trail, we reach a Y-junction 375 yards later (Wp.4 29M). For the linear stroll along **Lingmell Beck**, bear right here. For the full walk, we fork left and begin our long, steady climb, soon going through a gate

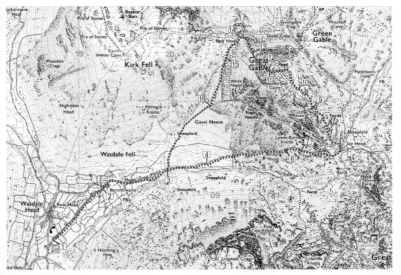

in a wall (Wp.5 37M), beyond which the gradient steepens. After crossing a watershed (Wp.6 59M), the path levels out briefly on a grassy knoll (Wp.7 64M), a good spot for a break if you wish to take it easy, which would seem eminently sensible given the outlook. Climbing resumes on a rougher, rockier path crossing a small crag before levelling off again and curving round a bend onto **Sty Head Pass**, where there are two forks to the left, just above the stretcher box (Wp.8 74M).

Kirk Fell & Great Gable

We turn left on the main path, the paved more northerly fork, which is framed by a couple of cairns. Climbing steadily (NW), we go through a shallow cleft at the head of a chute of red scree and pass below a small col (Wp.9 97M), another natural stopping point as there's a fine view over **Wast Water** from the grassy rise just a few yards above the path. The steady-to-steep climb continues on a tailored path traversing immense slopes of scree, gradually bearing round to a more westerly trajectory and passing the first of the cairns that guide us through the final climb (Wp.10 109M).

Picking our way across a sea of debris, we follow a rough way defined by large piles of stone, enjoying fine views of **Green Gable** and the northern **Lake District**, before a winding trodden way leads us onto the summit (Wp.11 122M).

Heading towards Buttermere

The summit is ringed with large cairns marking different descents. We aim for **Buttermere** (NW), bearing in mind that our real objective is marked by the plateau of **Kirk Fell** (W).

There are in fact a multiplicity of ways tending in this direction, none of them particularly easy in the initial descent. The larger cairns lead (NNW) to a reasonably stable but very obscure way down, the smaller (WNW) to a

Beck Head

clearer but more slippery path starting 75 yards from the summit (Wp.12).

Whichever of the parallel routes you opt for, avoid straying too far south as the slope becomes very steep and very slippery. After a painstaking time picking our way down the initial steep descent, we cross a scattering of solid rock patched with grass (Wp.13 142M), once again within sight of **Green Gable**. From here, we follow a more northerly, marginally gentler series of traverses down to the southern edge of a broad, slightly marshy shelf studded with old fencing posts (Wp.14 152M).

Descending into Wasdale

Bearing left, we descend (SW) toward **Wast Water** and the edge of **Beck Head** pass, crossing a marshy patch on the eastern side of the pass to join a clear path cutting across the scree on the western flank of **Great Gable** (Wp.15 158M). Ignoring the path-like erosion descending on our right toward the course of the beck, we stay on the main, flanking path, which is distinguished by a few roughly tailored steps and run-off channels.

We descend gently, then steadily (SSW) toward a distinct grassy shoulder that forms the left stroke of a V at the bottom of the beck, the right stroke being supplied by an erosion gully rising from the beck's right bank.

Resist the temptation to build up speed. There are places where stopping might prove problematic! At the top of the grassy shoulder, we cross a run-off channel and some tailored steps (Wp.16 171M). We now simply descend steeply along the grassy shoulder to rejoin our outward route at Wp.3 (190M).

The grassy shoulder descent

8 SCAFELL PIKE
via ESK HAUSE & LINGMELL

A small confession. I don't like culminating points. Too often, they're simply crowded and, in an emotional if not physical sense, anticlimactic. But one shouldn't succumb to prejudice, even one so arcane as 'bigism', and as England's highest summit, **Scafell Pike** can't really be ignored, especially given the astonishingly dramatic landscape in which it's set. In this itinerary, climbing the Pike provides the pretext for an eccentric ridge walk, the highest point merely acting as a peg on which we can hang visits to more interesting places. Given the rough traverse of **Broad Crag**, where the cairns are essential, and the long off-path section on **Lingmell**, good visibility is a vital prerequisite for taking any pleasure from this walk.

We start from the lay-by in front of the entrance to **Wasdale Head Hall Farm** and the National Trust car-park/campsite. There's room for a dozen vehicles in the lay-by, but it does fill up on a fine day, so you might be obliged to use the pay-and-display or re-jig the itinerary and start at the main (free) car-park further up the valley. If you're staying in the campsite, access is obvious. If you're staying further up the valley or parking at the main car-park, Wp.4 can be reached via the bridleway and footpath starting just south of the parking area (see Walk 10 Wp.5 for precise coordinates).

Access: on foot from **Wasdale**
Stroll: **Lingmell Beck**
Short Version: **Styhead Pass** returning via the ascent of Walk 7

We set off on the **Wasdale Head Hall Farm** driveway (Wp.1 0M), crossing the bridge then forking left into the campsite (Wp.2). Following the periphery track round the campsite, we exit via a gate/stile at the campsite's northeastern corner. 75 yards later, when the bridleway forks left to ford **Lingmell Beck**, we stay on the footpath on the left bank of the beck (Wp.3 6M).

Walking along a pebble dyke flanking the stream then on the grassy embankment of the beck, we follow a delightful path that doesn't appear on the maps, and which leads to a footbridge on the main path between the free car-park and the popular **Brown Tongue** ascent of **Scafell Pike** (Wp.4 17M). Staying on the left bank of the beck, we cross the main path and go through a small gate on the nearside of the bridge, maintaining our northeasterly direction on a narrow grassy path running parallel with the wall/fence above the stream.

Shadowing successive stretches of wall and fence along faint paths and sheep walks, we come to a stile (Wp.5 28M) opposite **Burnthwaite Farm**. Crossing the stile, we continue along the beck, passing several points where, on a warm day, there's a strong temptation to let the walking go hang and just lie in the river for a few hours. Presuming this temptation is resisted, we go through a kissing gate beside a footbridge (Wp.6). Ignoring the wayposted path

Plunge pool

crossing the bridge, we stay on the left bank of the beck, following a very faint sheep walk... so very faint, the remainder of the route to Wp.8 can effectively be considered off-path. Pathfinding, however, is not a problem, as we simply maintain direction (NE) alongside the beck, passing countless plunge pools and mini-races that are so appealing the compulsion to jump in is almost overpowering.

Soldiering on, we curve east, bringing **Great End** and the head of the valley into view. At this intermediate stage, such sheep walks as exist, are narrow and liable to be eclipsed in Summer by bracken, though the foliage is never so dense or extensive as to provoke any major anxieties about ticks or adders. We eventually pass a heart-shaped sheepfold (Wp.7 40M), after which we first have to negotiate a patch of very marshy ground and then withstand the blandishments of the most enticing plunge-pools yet. Approaching the confluence of **Lingmell Beck's** source streams, **Spouthead** and **Piers/Greta Gills**, we bear slightly right, crossing the broad sweep of boulders spanning the southernmost affluent (Wp.8 53M).

After picking our way across the boulders, we climb onto the spit dividing the feeder gills, where we join a faint path. Climbing (E) on an intermittently trodden way, we fork left after 75 yards at a faint Y-junction marked with a cairn on a boulder (Wp.9). An increasingly clear path then leads to a ford below the two watersheds feeding **Grainy Gill** (Wp.10 64M). Following a well defined path, we zigzag up the hillside to cross **Spouthead Gill** (Wp.11 75M), after which we bear right, guided by large cairns (E), onto one of two access paths for the popular **Corridor Route** to **Scafell Pike** (Wp.12 80M). Turning left, we climb to a pile of stones on the eastern edge of **Styhead Pass** (Wp.13 85M).

For the short version, turn left here then left again behind the stretcher box to

follow the ascent of Walk 7 back to **Wasdale Head**. For the full walk, we turn right on a broad, eroded trail climbing SE, passing after 200 yards a second access path onto the **Corridor Route** (Wp.14). Continuing on the main intermittently paved trail, we climb to **Sprinkling Tarn** (Wp.15 106M), which is a good place for a break as it's nobody's objective and, despite being so close to such a well-worn path, is a lovely peaceful spot.

Sprinkling Tarn

Suitably refreshed, we continue on the broad trail (SE), climbing gently below the impressive crags of **Great End**. After passing the **Ruddy Gill** path down to **Seathwaite** (Wp.16 115M), we climb more steadily to a Y-junction (Wp.17 120M), where we fork right on a broad, stony trail up to the **Esk Hause** intersection (Wp.18 129M).

Lingmell & Great Gable from near Wp.19

Turning right, we climb gently then steadily on a very broad trail leading to a massive pile of stones on the ridge between **Great End** and **Broad Crag** (Wp.19 141M), beyond which views open out across **Mosedale**.

Boulders mantle the next, unnamed rise, where our route is marked by large cairns at five to ten yard intervals, until the way levels off and becomes clearer again within sight of the distinctive circular dais crowning **Scafell Pike**.

After dipping down to a rocky col (Wp.20 156M), we're back on boulders again, clambering between cairns and skirting the summit of **Broad Crag**. We then descend again to a rough col, where we're joined by a precipitous branch of the **Corridor Route** and, on our left, the **Little Narrowcove** path (Wp.21 166M). Following a well worn path, we climb very steeply, then merely steeply to the dais and trig point on **Scafell Pike** (Wp.22 176M).

Once we've drunk in the views and resisted the temptation to cross **Broad Stand** onto **Sca Fell** summit (it looks easy but is well beyond the remit of this book), we follow the cairns (NW) onto a broad, stony trail. At a junction of cairn-marked ways 100 yards from the summit, we bear right (Wp.23) on the better trod way heading west. After a winding westerly descent, the trail veers right (Wp.24 190M) on a more northerly trajectory toward **Styhead Tarn**. Heading north then northwest, we descend to the junction with the main **Corridor Route** (Wp.25 198M).

It may seem sheerest folly to do any more climbing at this stage of the walk, especially given that the clear **Broad Tongue** trail descends directly to the left, but I strongly recommend making the extra effort to include **Lingmell** in the walk. It's a wonderful isolated little summit, infinitely more engaging than **Scafell Pike**, and for my money a strong candidate for the grandest view in the **Lake District**. What's more, you can almost guarantee you'll have it to yourself. A superb spot for a solitary picnic.

Turning right, we follow the **Corridor Route** for 25 yards then bear left, off-path, and head (NNW) toward **Lingmell** and a clear path that was discernible on the way down from **Scafell Pike**. Descending to cross a broken down wall, we pass a small pyramid cairn (Wp.26 204M), from where we simply climb NW onto the clear path. A steep but brief ascent, NW then N, brings us to the summit cairn on **Lingmell** (Wp.27 211M). Don't stop yet though!

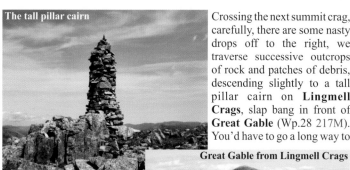
The tall pillar cairn

Crossing the next summit crag, carefully, there are some nasty drops off to the right, we traverse successive outcrops of rock and patches of debris, descending slightly to a tall pillar cairn on **Lingmell Crags**, slap bang in front of **Great Gable** (Wp.28 217M). You'd have to go a long way to

Great Gable from Lingmell Crags

encounter a more spectacular outlook.

Particularly horrifying (gratifying?) is the ghastly thread of the **South Traverse** cutting across the face of **Great Gable**.

We now take our cue from the large cairn to the left of the pillar and head west, descending (very much off-path) towards the low line of a tumbledown wall that lies to the right of the scree and debris spattered rise of **Goat Crags**. After descending across the scattered rocks immediately west of the pillar, we traverse a sloping pasture (WSW), briefly losing sight of both the wall and **Wast Water**. Curving below the northern tip of **Goat Crags**, we cross the wall beside a small cairn (Wp.29 229M) and bear right (W) passing a solitary pile of stones (Wp.30 232M). From the pile of stones, we resume a southwesterly trajectory, descending toward **Wast Water** on tufty, springy turf, to join a clear path a little way behind the grassy lip overlooking the lake (Wp.31 236M).

Bearing right, we follow this path (W) to a small pile of stones, from where we can see the campsite and the full length of **Wast Water** (Wp.32 239M). The next stretch of path, which appears to drop off into nowhere, has been badly eroded over the years, and is currently being landscaped and paved by the National Trust. At the time of writing, there is still one, unpleasantly skittery stretch, but by the time you read this, all the eroded slope should be paved where necessary, making for a well-graded, stable and spectacular descent that is far more enjoyable than the well known **Brown Tongue** route.

At the end of the projected tailored way, we descend steeply along a long grassy tongue to a ladder-stile (Wp.33 255M). Continuing our descent along the rapidly tapering tongue, we cross the path between **Brown Tongue** and the large parking area (Wp.34 262M). If you started from the large parking area, turn right here and descend to Wp.4. Otherwise, we maintain direction (W) toward **Wast Water**, eventually joining the main route at the tip of the tongue, where we go through a kissing gate (Wp.35 268M). 45 yards after the gate we cross a footbridge (Wp.36) and descend along the left bank of **Lingmell Gill**, rejoining the **Wasdale Head Hall Farm** track to return to our starting point.

9 YEWBARROW

I spent dark ages debating whether to include **Yewbarrow** in the **Mosedale Horseshoe** or make it a discrete itinerary, but eventually decided it's such a superb fell it merits a dedicated outing to itself, rather than simply being incorporated in a longer walk. This decision will not impress everyone. The day we recorded this itinerary, we met a woman who was climbing **Yewbarrow** and then going on to do the **Horseshoe**.... and then climbing **Kirk Fell**... and then climbing **Great Gable**.... and then climbing **Scafell Pike**... and then detouring to take in **Lord's Rake**, despite the fact that the rake is currently blocked by a dirty great boulder liable to render unto jam any rambler who happens to be in its path when it slips its moorings! Walkers of this stripe will reckon the present diddly little itinerary reeks of faintheartedness. But **Yewbarrow** is such a grand hill, boasting a rugged climb, precipitous slopes, impressive views, and an adventurous descent, I believe most will find it an extremely satisfying half-day excursion in its own right. Great, wild walking of incomparable drama. A summit to savour.

The top is exposed with steep slopes on all sides and not recommended in poor visibility or during strong winds. There is a risk of vertigo on the descent to **Dore Head**.

| 4 | 2½ H | 4.3 miles/7 km | 575m / 575m | ⟳ | ⚠ | 🍴 3 🔪 |

Access: by car. The walk starts from the **Overbeck Bridge** car-park, which is a little under a mile south of the National Trust campsite.

Yewbarrow from near the start

From the far end of the car park (Wp.1 0M), we take a clear path along the left bank of **Over Beck**, bearing right after a kissing-gate and climbing steeply to cross a stile (Wp.2 5M). Staying on the nearside of the fence at a second stile 50 yards later, we climb steeply

View approaching Wp.3

alongside the fence, eventually crossing a ladder-stile over a wall at the foot of the crags (Wp.3 22M).

75 yards after the stile, we fork right at a Y-junction (Wp.4). Following a rough but clear path, we climb to a brief paved section, where we veer right, away from a long erosion scar (Wp.5 29M). The path is slightly obscure here, but reasonably easy to follow, and easily confirmed by a glance over the shoulder, as the zigzags

are obvious from above. A steep, rough climb brings us to the head of the erosion scar, opposite a short wall and at the foot of the **Great Door** gully (Wp.6 40M).

We can either scramble straight up the gully or use marginally easier ways shadowing its western flank, though most people will favour a combination of the two, initially in the gully then on its flank when it steepens

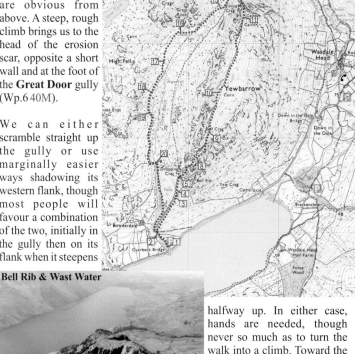

Bell Rib & Wast Water

halfway up. In either case, hands are needed, though never so much as to turn the walk into a climb. Toward the top, as the gully bears right and becomes a chute of scree, we emerge beside a cairn at the base of a long slope carpeted with blueberry and heather (Wp.7 47M).

Clambering over the crag

We continue climbing steeply on a rough, scree-patched path that joins the ridge above a precipitous slope descending toward **Wast Water** (Wp.8 54M) - not wildly vertiginous, but it appears very abruptly. Bearing left, we follow the crest to the north, clambering over a rugged crag onto grassy uplands, reaching the **Bull Crag** summit cairn 250 yards later (Wp.9). From here, easy strolling along the heights takes us past a second summit cairn (Wp.10) to a large pile of stones above **Stirrup Crag** (Wp.11 84M).

The views from **Stirrup Crag** are stunning. So is the descent to **Dore Head**, the top of which is marked by a smaller cairn 45 yards to the north. Arms and bottoms are necessary, bulky rucksacks eminently expendable, as there are at least two points where we have to lever ourselves round, down and over rough rocks. Happily, the footing is firm for the most part and the way down proves easier than it looks. Still, at the risk of sounding fatuous, take it one step at a time.

Slithering down the crevice (Wp.12)

The first tricky section comes 100 yards from the large pile of stones, at a point where we have to slither down a shallow crevice (Wp.12) - this can be skirted to the right, but it's more precipitous that way, so I recommend sticking with the crevice. 25 yards after that, we pass a pile of stones on a sloping rock and descend to a small cairn (Wp.13) where we bear left, edging round a rock for another bottom-slither, after which we join a clear, stony path. Worth turning back here to try and work out where on earth you descended. Now it's a comparatively simple matter of following the eroded way zigzagging down to **Dore Head** (Wp.14 101M).

Bearing left, we head SW then S, initially on a clear path that eventually leads back to Wp.4, but soon bearing right, off-path, to pass between two massive boulders (Wp.15 104M) and cross onto the right bank of the spring at the head of **Over Beck**. Maintaining direction (SW), still off-path on spongy springy turf, we cross a second feeder spring, after which an infinitely faint way winds through scattered rocks. The way becomes marginally clearer as it approaches a tiny grassy hummock with a horn of rock on its left hand side, behind which we curve west to avoid a boggy depression below the hummock.

After crossing a third feeder spring (Wp.16 113M), the faint way follows a contour curving round the boggy depression (SW then S), then gradually begins descending, crossing a fourth feeder (Wp.17 118M). The way becomes obscure again here, but maintaining a southerly direction and occasionally contouring round waterlogged land, we soon find ourselves following a faint but discernible way again, cutting through sparse bracken and passing a large cairn on a flat rock (Wp.18 125M). 200 yards later, we descend to a footbridge over **Brimfull Beck** and join a clear path (Wp.19 129M).

After a gentle stroll along the clear path, we descend alongside a wall to a footbridge crossing **Over Beck**, immediately after which we bear right (Wp.20 138M), traversing a patch of marshy ground to pick up a narrow path through the bracken. The path passes a precipitous drop over a spectacular little waterfall then curves round to go through a gate, rejoining our outward route between the kissing gate and the stile.

Climbing mountains can be a humbling experience, cutting mere human beings down to size and withering the best fed ego. But sometimes the sheer magnitude of it all, the breadth and depth and elevation of the outlook, can have the opposite effect, expanding being into something bigger and better than is viable in the space available at lower altitudes. This probably isn't a very healthy sensation, but like many unhealthy sensations, it's the most tremendous fun. If ever a walk were designed to give you a grand and godlike feeling, the **Mosedale Horseshoe** is it. Entering the great basin of **Mosedale**, you feel like you're being cradled in the palm of a giant's baseball glove. Once on top, you get the distinct impression you have become that giant. Go, flatter yourself, be big!

5   4.7 H   10.3 miles/16½km   970m   970m   3

Access: on foot from **Wasdale**

| **Stroll** |
| **Mosedale** (see text) |

We start from the lay-by parking area in front of the National Trust car-park/campsite, though the route can be joined at the larger free parking area near the inn or at the inn itself, both of which are passed en route.

We set off on the **Wasdale Head Hall Farm** driveway (Wp.1 0M), crossing the bridge then forking left into the campsite (Wp.2). Following the periphery track round the campsite, we exit via a gate/stile at the campsite's north-eastern corner. 75-yards later, when the bridleway forks left to ford **Lingmell Beck**, we stay on the footpath on the left bank of the beck (Wp.3 6M). Walking along a pebble dyke flanking the stream then on the grassy embankment of the beck, we come to a footbridge (Wp.4 13M).

The Horseshoe from Lingmell Crags

Approaching the Inn

Crossing the bridge, we cut across pasture (NW) to rejoin the road just south of the main free parking area (Wp.5 17M). Turning right, we follow the road to the 'Inn', then turn left in front of the **Barn Door Shop** (Wp.6 23M), and follow the signs for 'Black Sail Pass', which lead us onto a grassy trail along the left bank (our right) of the stream behind the pub.

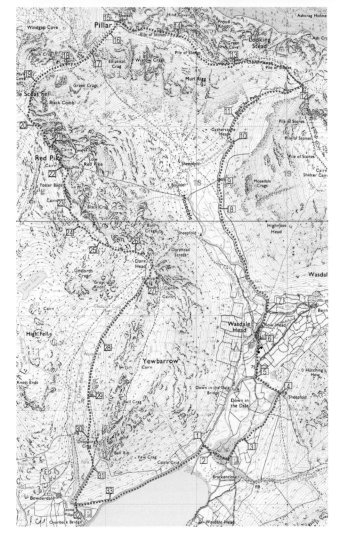

Mosedale

At a Y-junction immediately after the confluence of **Mosedale** and **Fogmire Becks**, we fork left (Wp.7 28M). Staying on the main trail and ignoring (most emphatically ignoring; it looks awful!) the punishing drag up **Kirk Fell** to our right, we cross a small rise, bringing into view the full sweep of **Mosedale**. Easy walking takes us deep into the dale, where we pass a large pile of stones, immediately after which we ignore a faint fork off to the left (Wp.8 47M).

If you're doing the stroll, you might like to branch off here to find a picnic spot toward the head of the dale.

For the full walk, we stay on the main trail as it veers north, climbing to a gate in a wall (Wp.9 52M), after which we bear NE, the gradient steepening as we approach a ford across **Gatherstone Beck** (Wp.10 63M). The steady climb continues, briefly in a westerly direction, but soon resumes a NE trajectory, crossing a grassy rise where the path levels off at a paved run-off channel (Wp.11 72M). This is a welcome respite since, 200 yards later, the steep climbing resumes for the final paved haul up to **Black Sail Pass**, where we turn left to follow (WNW) a line of rusting fence posts (Wp.12 94M).

Posts and path diverge then briefly converge again at the base of the first crags, where we reach a triple junction (Wp.13 111M). The large cairn on the right marks the climbers' path to **Pillar Rock**. The way straight ahead is an eminently missable shortcut. We fork left, enjoying great views over **Mosedale** and the blade-like rise of **Yewbarrow** while climbing steadily on a rough but clear path that soon crosses the line of fencing posts again.

Pillar from Red Pike

Leaving the posts to our right, we climb onto a grassy plateau, where we curve NW toward the rocky rise of the unnamed 853-metre summit, below which path and posts converge again (Wp.14 128M). A steady climb across stony ground between the fencing posts and large cairns leads to a dramatic ridge punctuated by small pointed crags then up again to the small plateau and trig-point of **Pillar** summit (Wp.15 143M).

Our onward route (SW) is indicated by a line of cairns, notably two large ones, the second of which (Wp.16, 125 yards from the trig-point) marks the start of our first descent. Picking our way across a clear, stony way, we descend steadily then steeply; some care required on the loose stones, to **Wind Gap**, where there's an escape route into **Mosedale** across the scree to our left (Wp.17 155M). Maintaining direction (SW), we climb onto **Black Crag**, the boulder strewn summit of which is capped with a large cairn (Wp.18 164M).

We now stretch our legs out for an agreeable stroll across grassy uplands to a Y-junction (Wp.19 170M). Peak-baggers may care to follow the faint branch to the right onto **Scoat Fell** and **Steeple**, otherwise we bear left, staying on the main path as it follows a contour, gradually curving ESE to the foot of the last climb of the day, a comparatively gentle ascent along the back of **Red Pike** (Wp.20 177M).

Red Pike

Following a clear path breached by occasional jumbles of rock, we climb to a Y-junction (Wp.21 183M). Either branch will do, and the gently ascending route directly ahead looks temptingly easy, but for better views I recommend forking left on the cairn-marked route across the rocks to follow a rough path hugging the rim of the horseshoe. The path peters out after passing a large cairn on the highest point of **Red Pike** (Wp.22 190M), but we simply cut across the grassy heights, rejoining the easy path shortly before a second large cairn on the edge of a wasteland of debris and desiccated lichen (Wp.23 197M).

Ignoring, if you happen to see them, several large cairns to the south, we descend (SE) to the left of the rocks, following a grassy slope that is soon scarred by an eroded path, heading for the insane looking descent off **Yewbarrow** - if you haven't done it (see Walk 9), it's via the rocks above the squiggly, eroded path directly ahead. Our path bears south briefly, bringing into view **Wast Water**, before veering ESE again (Wp.24 206M), descending onto a broad, shelf-like pasture, apparently flat from above, but in fact a slope. Toward the lip of the 'shelf', we fork right on a cairn-marked way (Wp.25 211M) and descend steadily across a succession of giant's steps. The 'steps' end at **Dore Head**, where the eroded way dwindles to a grassy path a little way short of a brown scar in the peat which, from above, resembles a cross (Wp.26 224M).

On the far side of the pass, at the foot of the **Yewbarrow** descent, we bear right (S), onto a grassy path passing to the left of two massive boulders (Wp.27 229M). Though occasionally faint and intermittently boggy to begin with, this path is easy to follow as it curves along a contour, soon bringing **Wast Water** back into view (Wp.28 241M). Following an increasingly clear path, we pass below a small outcrop of rock and cross a meagre affluent of **Over Beck** (Wp.29 249M). We then descend to a broken wall, though this is currently being repaired lower down, and looks like it may well soon have a fence and gate at the top (Wp.30 256M). 325 yards later, we cross a ladder-stile in a wall and turn right (Wp.31 260M). After a steep descent alongside a fence, we turn sharp left in front of the second of two stiles at the bottom of the fence (Wp.32 269M). Following a well-trodden right-of-way cutting across the lower slopes of **Yewbarrow** (E), we cross a stile and join the road (Wp.33 274M) a little over half a mile from our starting point.

11 SEATHWAITE TARN & THE RIVER DUDDON

Wordsworth spoke of the **Duddon Valley** as a place possessing "a harmony of tone and colour, a consummation and perfection of beauty, which would have been marred had aim or purpose intervened with the course of convenience, utility or necessity". Often enough, such romantic rhapsodies are a herald of disappointment for the modern walker, but not so in **Dunnerdale**, which to this day remains refreshingly free of "aim or purpose". **Seathwaite Tarn** is a lovely place with a distinctly Pyrenean feel to it, and the walk down the **River Duddon** is so wonderfully varied, involving gentle strolling, lively little stretches of scrambling over rocks, and all manner of woodland, you could happily carry on following the river all the way to the estuary. Not possible, I'm afraid, but then there's no great hardship to ending a walk at the excellent **Newfield Inn**.

3	3½ H	7.1 miles/11½km		220m 220m		5

Access: on foot from **Seathwaite**

Stroll
Memorial Bridge and **Wallowbarrow Gorge** (see text)
Short Version
Wallowbarrow Gorge in reverse (see text)

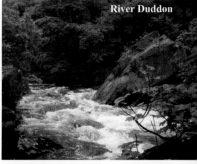

River Duddon

Starting from parking area just past **Seathwaite Church** (Wp.1 0M), we follow the road up the valley, passing **Turner Hall Farm**, **Under Crag**, the **Walna Scar** 'Coniston' turn-off, and a public footpath on the right just before **Seathwaite Bridge**. Immediately after the bridge, we leave the road, turning right on a signposted footpath skirting an area of marsh on the banks of **Tarn Beck** (Wp.2 10M).

Duck boards take us across the marsh to a stile, after which more duck boards lead to a gate just short of a ruin (Wp.3 16M). Ignoring the permissive path that goes through the gate for 'Duddon Road', we turn right, climbing alongside a fence onto level ground curving round to a junction (Wp.4 21M). Once again ignoring the left fork, which also leads to the road, we bear right on a path signposted 'Alternative Drier Route', skirting the marsh and crossing a waymarked ladder-stile (Wp.5 23M).

A lovely fern lined path winds through woodland, passing behind a farm building and a cottage before going through a gate, immediately after which we turn right to cross a footbridge and ladder-stile (Wp.6 33M). We then bear left (ENE) on a rough intermittent trail going through another gate and crossing a gate/ladder-stile (Wp.7 40M).

We now climb toward the wall on our right on a faint but broad and easily

discernible trail. After climbing steadily along the nearside of the wall (NE), we follow then cross an affluent of the main beck (Wp.8 53M), above which the gradient eases for the final approach to the main track between **Walna Scar Road** and the tarn (Wp.9 57M).

Seathwaite Tarn

Turning left, we follow the track to **Seathwaite Tarn** and the southern end of the dam wall (Wp.10 64M).

In fine weather, it's possible to circle the tarn using faint paths and sheep walks, rejoining the described route at Wp.11. Otherwise, we simply cross the dam wall and the sluice gates at its far end then bear left (Wp.11 69M) for an essentially off-path descent crossing a broad area of marsh, favouring the higher, drier ground on the right below **Burnt Crag**.

350 yards from the dam wall we join a broad, grassy trail (Wp.12 74M), which we follow (SW) down to a faint Y-junction (Wp.13 78M) where we fork right, climbing slightly (NW) to avoid more marshy ground. The path bears west and we descend to cross a tiny brook, 20 yards after which a small waypost (Wp.14 83M) indicates where we turn left, heading south for 75 yards to a second waypost and a clear grassy path descending in a westerly direction.

This path gradually curves north and goes through a gate (Wp.15 92M). Descending across a maze of crisscrossing sheep walks, we aim for a narrow path (clearly visible from above) climbing from a breach in a wall to a stile over a fence (Wp.16 100M). Maintaining a northerly direction after the stile, we follow a faint sheep walk down to a ladder stile into the woods around **Hinning House Close** (Wp.17 106M). Once again on a clear path, we head NNE, skirting behind fire-damaged woodland to join the **Duddon** road (Wp.18 110M).

Turning left, we follow the road for 15 yards, then descend into the **Birks Bridge** car park and cross the bridge, immediately after which we turn left on a wayposted bridleway (Wp.19 113M). Ignoring a stile on our right 100 yards later, we cross a tiny footbridge then bear left on a dirt track (Wp.20) leading back to another bridge over the river, just before which, we turn right to join a wayposted path along the right bank of the river. The remainder of the walk is waymarked at all key junctions, so I recommend putting the book away and just enjoying the walking.

Following the wayposted path, we fork left at a junction of paths (Wp.21 124M), threading our way through the delightful **Great Wood** and crossing a duck board that can be extremely slippery. After crossing a stile, the waymarking guides us up through the woods to emerge above the main growth of trees on an outcrop of rock. We descend directly to an area of cleared woodland, where we turn left (Wp.22 135M) back toward the river and **Troutal Bridge**. Staying on the right bank of the river, we follow the waymarked route as it bears away from the river, traversing a dense pine wood (GPS reception doesn't quite disappear here, but it's a near thing). The waymarked route returns to the riverbank at a point where the pine give way to beech (Wp.23 151M), then meanders along the narrow border between the woods and the water. Shortly after fording an affluent (Wp.24 156M) we pass stepping stones (invisible when the river's in spate) and a steel cable 'handrail' stretched across the river.

Once again, we stay on the right bank, soon crossing a footbridge over **Grassguards Gill** (Wp.25 163M), immediately after which we bear right, climbing to avoid boggy ground. After passing a rocky knoll overlooking **Wallowbarrow Crag** (Wp.26 170M) (a good objective for a long stroll in reverse), we dip into lovely, lush woodland, great banks of fern carpeting the flanks of the valley below a loosely woven canopy of oak leaves. We then traverse a major, 750 yard long rockslide, which can be quite heavy going when the rocks are wet.

Memorial Footbridge

Beyond the rockslide, the valley broadens, offering abundant picnic spots amid the oaks which would be suitable for a short stroll, as we approach the **Memorial Footbridge** (Wp.27 196M). On the far side of the bridge, we have a choice of routes. The first, though slightly longer and involving a little road walking, is the more attractive and is recommended after wet weather when the second, more direct option can be horribly muddy.

1. Immediately after crossing the bridge, we turn right and follow the left bank of the river for 175 yards before forking left to cross a footbridge over **Tarn Beck**, rejoining the **Duddon** road 100 yards south of the pub.

2. Alternatively, to go directly to the pub or the parking area, we carry straight ahead after the bridge and follow a marginally less attractive path, leading to a signposted junction 75 yards short of the road, where we can bear right to emerge directly in front of the pub or left to go to the parking area.

Patterned with the spoil of a clean cut forest, the base of **Harter Fell** can look a little dispiriting, but one should not be put off by this initially forbidding aspect, for the summit itself is a splendid little elevation with fabulous views encompassing **Eskdale**, **Wasdale**, **Bow Fell**, **Crinkle Crags**, the **Coniston Fells** and, on a clear day, the **Isle of Man**. The climb is steep, so despite its brevity the itinerary earns a high exertion rating, but it's highly recommended, especially for those intent on the pathless ascent of **Grey Friars** (Walk 13), and for anyone wishing to have a look at **Hardknott Pass** without the usual clutch-frazzling, temper-fraying manoeuvres.

4 | 2 H | 4.1 miles/6.6 km | 463m / 463m | ↻ | 3

Access: by car or (limited service) bus from Ulverston

Stroll
Dunnerdale Forest (see text)

The entrance to the car park

We start from the **Birks Bridge Forestry Commission** car park toward the head of the **Duddon Valley** (Wp.1 0M). Crossing the bridge over the **River Duddon**, we fork left after 150 yards (Wp.2), staying on the main dirt track as it climbs toward **Birks Farm**, soon crossing a rough forestry track marked with a bridleway waypost (Wp.3 8M).

Climbing across the clear cut

40 yards after passing a fork on the left down to the farm, we leave the track, turning right on a narrow path marked with a stumpy signpost for 'Harter Fell' (Wp.4 11M). Taking the right hand fork at a second stumpy signpost 75 yards from the track (Wp.5), we begin our steep climb, crossing the scar of an abandoned forestry track 125 yards later.

Following a rough path marked with intermittent and rather provisional looking orange-tipped wayposts, we pick our way across a boulder-strewn watershed (Wp.6 20M). After climbing very steeply alongside the watershed for 175 yards, we cross its subterranean head (Wp.7 29M) to 'emerge' above the quondam treeline.

Climbing less steeply on a clearer path, we traverse more attractive heathland to a gate in a fence (Wp.8 38M). This is a good spot to stop and have a look at the **Coniston Fells**. **Grey Friar** is the summit to the left of **Seathwaite Tarn**. In Walk 13, we take the obvious track climbing from the south to the dam wall,

then follow the spur defining the northwestern shoulder of the cirque.

For the present itinerary, we maintain our northerly direction on a faint grassy path climbing between the visible crags (not the summit!), behind which we join a broad trail climbing from the northeast (Wp.9 50M), 150 yards from the trig point on **Harter Fell** (Wp.10 53M). Since there's no ridge for enjoying the views as you walk, it's worth stopping here to take in the grand display of the surrounding mountains and the somewhat sorrier spectacle of toy cars inching their way up (or possibly not as the case may be) **Hardknott Pass**.

The pass on the summit

To descend, we double back to the obvious, broad pass slicing through the scattered summit crags, and head west on a broad trail toward **Muncaster Fell** and the **Isle of Man**. At a Y-junction just below the summit (Wp.11 55M), we fork left on a narrow path heading towards **Green Crag**. After a steady then steep descent, the path crosses a sheep-walk (Wp.12 66M) and we stroll across gently sloping grassland onto soggier ground where the trodden way grows indistinct.

Following a succession of natural meanders winding through the rocks, we soon recover a clear, dry path descending toward the new plantation on the edge of **Dunnerdale Forest**. We stay on the clear path as it bears right to pass behind the plantation fence, then descend alongside the northern limit of the fence to a pedestrian gate (Wp.13 77M).

Going through the gate, we follow a distinct, but muddy and slightly muddled trail, weaving through woods of frothy young pine with clusters of birch saplings staking a claim to the damper ground. After 450 yards traversing the new plantation, we bear left at a waypost (Wp.14 86M) and emerge on the turning circle at the end of the track climbing from **Birks Bridge**. This would be a possible objective for a stroll, forking left at Wp.5 and following the end of the walk in reverse.

From the turning circle, we follow the track for 750 yards until a sharp right-hand bend (Wp.15 97M), where we fork left, maintaining an easterly direction on an unmarked path cutting across the cleared forest. We now simply follow this path/trail, which is reasonably clear apart from a couple of boggy bits, rejoining our outward route at Wp.5 (109M).

The **Old Man** of **Coniston** is usually approached, logically enough, from **Coniston**, but we've opted for this less well known route for a number of reasons. First, it's as off the beaten path as you get in the **Coniston Fells**; second, it's more satisfying than the obvious up and down routes; third, it offers a beguiling perspective on the magnificent cirque cradling **Seathwaite Tarn**; and fourth, it includes both the comparatively little visited summit of **Grey Friar** and the dramatic cliffs of **Dow Crag**. Though there is a faint trodden way, the ascent of **Grey Friar** is more or less off-path, certainly off any path appearing on the maps, but so long as visibility is good you shouldn't encounter any problems and, if visibility is poor, there isn't a huge amount of point doing the walk anyway!

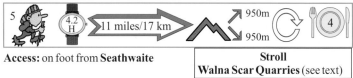

Access: on foot from **Seathwaite**

Stroll
Walna Scar Quarries (see text)

Starting from the small car park immediately north of **Seathwaite** church (Wp.1 0M), we walk up the road to the **Turner Hall Farm** driveway (Wp.2). Turning right then forking left through the **High Moss** gate 50 yards later (Wp.3), we follow a waymarked footpath through a second gate (Wp.4). Following the track on the left across a field, we pass to the left of **High Moss** house, behind which we go through a third gate and cross a field spiked with marsh grass to join the lower, asphalted stretch of the **Walna Scar** Road (Wp.5 15M). Turning right, to pass **Beck House**, we follow the lane to a Y-junction at the end of the tarmac (Wp.6 19M).

The Scafells from Walna Scar road

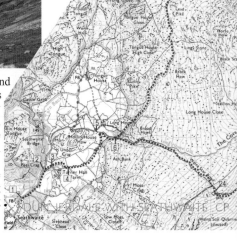

Though parking's limited and manoeuvering tricky, this point can also be reached by car, taking the first road on the right after **Seathwaite** (signed 'Coniston unsuitable for vehicles'). For the stroll, stay on the main track here climbing along the left bank of **Long**

House Gill. The **Walna Scar** quarry ruins (obvious from below thanks to the mounds of spoil), which have good views of the **Scafells** and would make a nice picnic spot on a fine day, are reached by a path on the right (Wp.24) shortly after the **Walna Scar** Road has gone through a second gateway. Alternatively, there are numerous pleasant picnic spots along the gill's banks.

For the full walk, we fork left at the end of the tarmac, crossing a bridge to climb gently on a pleasant grassy track with fine views of the **Scafells**. We follow this track all the way to **Seathwaite Tarn**, where a spur climbs onto the end of the dam wall (Wp.7 45M). After crossing the dam wall and the sluice gates at its northern end, we follow a grassy path north for 75 yards to a very faint Y-junction (Wp.8 51M) just before the half-moon scar of what appears to have been a shallow quarry.

Our next objective is the flattest, least rocky part of the ridge on our left. Forking left, we climb steadily to steeply along the faint trodden way (NNE), which is relatively easy to follow as it adheres to a natural line of ascent onto **Troutal Fell**, reaching the back of the ridge beside a small white rock (Wp.9 67M). Bearing right, still following a faint trodden way, we make our way along the ridge (NE), weaving between tiny outcrops of fissured rock, opting for the higher ground if the way seems in doubt. After an initially gentle climb, the ascent steepens on **Wether How** (Wp.10 81M) for the final haul to the summit cairn on **Grey Friar** (Wp.11 90M).

Heading ENE across the plateau beyond the summit cairn, we soon pick up a clear path descending (ENE) to a distinct triple fork directly behind the **Carrs** (Wp.12 99M).

If you've not visited the **Carrs** and **Swirl How** or

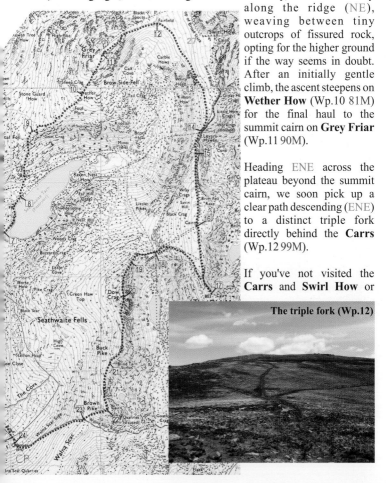

The triple fork (Wp.12)

don't intend doing Walk 22, carry straight ahead on the central fork then follow the 'motorway' trail along the ridge to rejoin the described route at Wp.14. Otherwise, we fork right on a clear path curving ESE, passing above small crags (Wp.13 111M) before joining the main, eroded ridge trail just above **Levers Hawse** col (Wp.14 118M).

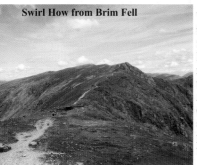
Swirl How from Brim Fell

We now follow the main 'motorway' trail (SW) and, ignoring a minor path forking right across the flank of **Brim Fell** (Wp.15), climb steadily, passing numerous large piles of stone as we traverse the bare dome of **Brim Fell**. After the **Brim Fell** summit cairn (Wp.16 136M), a straightforward stroll leads us onto the **Old Man** promontory, at the end of which is the trig point (Wp.17 146M).

Chances are it'll be elbow room only on the summit, but you can understand why the **Old Man** is such a grand old man: **Duddon Sands**, **Morecombe Bay**, the fields, lakes and forests of southern Lakeland, and beyond the Dales, meld in a glorious abstract of colour, shade and light. And the best is yet to come!

Retracing our steps some 100 yards from the **Old Man** trig point, we take another obvious 'motorway' trail down to **Goat's Hawse** and the junction with another of the popular tourist paths climbing from **Coniston** (Wp.18 157M). We maintain direction (W) on a broad naturally paved trail climbing steadily before curving south (Wp.19 163M) to follow a less distinct cairn-marked way traversing jagged rocks to the very craggy (think ageing Hollywood matinee idol) **Dow Crag**, the basin-like summit of which is reached by a brief, hands-on scramble (Wp.20 174M).

Blind Tarn

From the summit, we follow a broad but not excessively wide trail traversing rough ground along the edge of the ragged ridge, passing some spectacular clefts with views onto **Goat's Water** and **Coniston Water**. The trail widens as it drops down to a level stretch overlooking **Blind Tarn** (Wp.21 189M).

After crossing the green swathed rise of **Brown** (sic) **Pike** (Wp.22 196M), we descend steadily on a broad stony trail (SW) to join the **Walna Scar** Road, at this stage a rough eroded track (Wp.23 202M). Turning right, we follow the track back to rejoin our outward route at Wp.6, passing en route a path heading south into the **Walna Scar** quarry ruins (Wp.24 212M).

14 SILVER HOW, BLEA RIGG, & STICKLE TARN

A low level walk with high level views. Also a good way of getting away from the crowds, since the chances are you'll have the greater part of the uplands to yourself, except perhaps at weekends when the odd guided party uses **Blea Rigg** as an approach route for **Sergeant Man**. Not recommended when visibility is poor as **Silver How** is a maze of crisscrossing sheep walks, but otherwise very easy, only earning a 3 exertion rating for the steep climb near the beginning. We start from one of our accommodation suggestions, **Baysbrown Farm Campsite**, but the itinerary can easily be joined in **Chapel Stile** or at **Dungeon Ghyll** if you're staying there. If you're arriving by car, there is very limited free parking in **Chapel Stile** and a large 'Pay & Display' at **Dungeon Ghyll**.

3 | 3.7 H | 7.7 miles/12 km | 500m / 500m | ↻ | 4

Access: on foot from **Chapel Stile** or **Dungeon Ghyll***

* For bus information see Appendices

Short Version Stickle Tarn from **Dungeon Ghyll**

From the T-junction with the track leading up to the **Baysbrown Farm** buildings (Wp.1 0M), we follow the main access track to **Chapel Stile**. As we approach the village, we can see our grassy path climbing the hillside to the right of the church tower.

Chapel Stile

After turning right on the B5343 (Wp.2 7M), we take the main lane through **Chapel Stile**, passing below the church. The lane passes three pedestrian gates in the fence on our left (alternative ways onto the fell), but we stay on the lane till it passes **Speddy** and **End** cottages, where we fork left on a signposted footpath (Wp.3 15M) climbing to the east.

At a junction (Wp.4 23M) opposite **Banks Quarry** (the working quarry visible on the far side of the valley), we bear left for a brief but steep climb (NE) to a crossroads of paths (partially disguised from below by a Y-junction; Wp.5 31M). Turning left, we follow a narrow path winding along the ridge, bringing **Grasmere** and **Fairfield** into view as we cross a level area where we come to a confluence of ways (Wp.6 38M). Forking right, we take the stony, cairn-marked way climbing through low crags to a chest-high cairn (Wp.7 45M). Maintaining a northerly direction, we climb across a map-defying maze of grassy paths to a second large cairn on the heights to the southwest of **Silver How** (Wp.8 53M).

Continuing to the north, essentially off-path for the moment, we meander across rolling pasture, enjoying fine views of the **Langdale Pikes**. On the rise above the basin of **Brigstone Moss**, we recover a faint trodden way (Wp.9 61M) descending NNW to join a clear path beside a cairn below **Lang How Crag** (Wp.10 65M). Following the clear path north, we curve round a grassy dome

Great Langdale

tipped with a nipple-like cairn, after which we cross two dips in the ridge, reaching a Y-junction in the second dip (Wp.11 78M). We can take either path as they rejoin after the next hummock to form a broad cairn-marked trail.

This trail climbs steadily to a shallow declivity alongside **Little Castle How** before descending briefly to another junction (Wp.12 90M), where we can again take either route as they soon rejoin to form a well stabilized path traversing a plateau spotted with tiny tarns and patches of marsh.

The improvised shelter at Wp.15

At the westernmost tarn (Wp.13 101M), the path bears southwest briefly, skirting the first rise of **Blea Rigg**, and we pass a pathless, cairn-marked route descending on our right to **Easedale Tarn** (Wp.14 105M). The tarn itself comes into view a few yards later as we climb along a clear path winding through the rocks and passing a small improvised shelter (Wp.15 112M).

We then swing north briefly, bringing into view the diminutive **Codale Tarn** and the full sweep of the high mountains encircling **Great Langdale** as we traverse the marshy uplands of **Blea Rigg** (N).

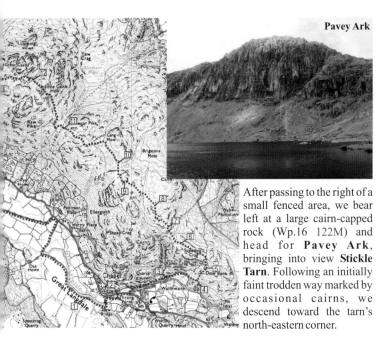

Pavey Ark

After passing to the right of a small fenced area, we bear left at a large cairn-capped rock (Wp.16 122M) and head for **Pavey Ark**, bringing into view **Stickle Tarn**. Following an initially faint trodden way marked by occasional cairns, we descend toward the tarn's north-eastern corner.

The path gradually becomes clearer, meandering round a patchwork of marshland before drawing alongside **Stickle Tarn** (Wp.17 139M). Behind the tarn is the famous **Jack's Rake**, a Grade 1 scramble across the face of **Pavey Ark**. You should be able to pick it out by the bright necklace of hikers strung along the cliff and a few dozen more queuing (!) at the bottom to get on it.

Turning left, we walk alongside the tarn and follow the broad, eroded trail descending along the left bank of **Stickle Ghyll**, which is less crowded than the main route on the right bank. The trail crosses a grassy rise then feeds into a roughly paved branch of the main trail (Wp.18 151M). After a steep descent, we join the main trail beside a slate footbridge (Wp.19 165M) and turn left to descend to the principal car park, **Sticklebarn Inn** and **New Dungeon Ghyll Hotel**.

From the left hand corner of the smaller car park on the far side of the road (Wp.20 183M), we take a farm track to the east. When the track rejoins the road (204M), we turn right and follow the road for 40 yards then turn right again on another track down to **Great Langdale Beck**. After crossing a bridge, we turn left (210M) and follow the **Cumbria Way** track back to our starting point.

The straggledy rise of **Lingmoor Fell** is often ignored in the race to reach the **Langdale Pikes** and **Crinkle Crags**, which is a pity, as it's a great walk on rugged ground with wonderful views, and is generally accessible during Winter when ice and snow deter all but the most determined walkers from tackling the higher summits.

The described itinerary starts from **Baysbrown Campsite**, but can easily be joined from **Chapel Stile** village or **Great Langdale**. To reach the start from **Chapel Stile**, take the footpath at Wp.19 or, if you're staying further up the road, go directly to the signposted track into **Baysbrown Campsite**. If you're staying in **Great Langdale** or are arriving by car, take the signposted footpath just west of the small 'Pay & Display' car park in front of **Sticklebarn Tavern** and **New Dungeon Ghyll Hotel** to join the described route at Wp.4. The path can also be joined (see text) from **Great Langdale** Campsite. See the Appendices for details of access by bus from **Ambleside**.

Access: on foot from Chapel Stile or Great Langdale	**Strolls**
	(a) Chapel Stile to **Great Langdale**, crossing the footbridge at Wp.4 and returning via the tracks detailed at the end of Walk 14
	(b) Baysbrown Wood from **Chapel Stile** in reverse

From the T-junction with the track leading to the farm buildings in **Baysbrown Farm Campsite** (Wp.1 0M), we take the **Cumbria Way** track towards **Great Langdale**, passing in front of **Oak Howe** cottage, behind which we fork right at a junction of paths (Wp.2 9M).

This delightful path climbs gently, curving round to the west with clear views of the principal routes up the **Langdale Pikes** and bringing into view directly ahead of us the mini-peak of **Side Pike**. After going through a corner gate in a sheepfold (Wp.3 24M), we descend on a paved trail to a footbridge behind **Side House Farm** (Wp.4 31M). Without crossing the footbridge, we bear left, crossing a second footbridge above the farm and going over a ladder-stile.

Side Pike

We then follow a well trodden trail traversing the gently sloping pasture below **Side Pike** before contouring round the hillside above the National Trust campsite (50 yards above a gate in the campsite's southeastern corner). When the path loses definition behind the campsite, we climb slightly, skirting behind a conifer wood to go through a kissing gate at the western limit of the pasture (Wp.5 45M).

Curving left, we climb steadily alongside a wall on an eroded path (accessible from the campsite's southwestern corner) leading to a rise overlooking **Blea Tarn** beside a ladder stile and a cattle grid on the minor, western road between the two **Langdales** (Wp.6 63M). Without crossing the stile, we stay on the eastern side of the road, following a contour curving below **Side Pike**.

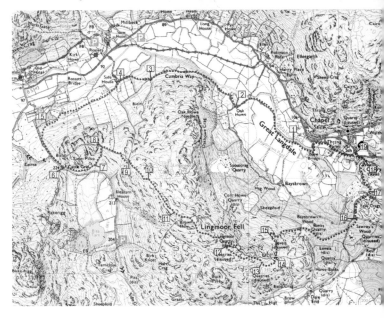

After crossing a conventional stile (Wp.7 70M), we turn left and climb steeply to the col just east of **Side Pike** (Wp.8 77M). If this ascent seems onerous, spare a thought for Sam and Charlie, two boys who tackled it the day we recorded the route. Their ages? Three and four!

Hailstorm approaching from the north

Bearing right, we climb alongside a wall, then cross a stile in a fence below the first crags (Wp.9 86M). Turning right, we climb across rocks to follow the continuation of the wall. A rough but easy climb on a good dry path skirts to the right of a first crag silhouetted against the skyline then curves onto the back of the ridge beside a cairn (Wp.10 92M). We continue along the fence/wall (SE), bringing into view **Lingmoor Tarn** before crossing the first of twin summits on **Brown How** (Wp.11 101M), from where we can see **Chapel Stile**.

Continuing along the fence/wall, we can cross onto its western side at the second summit, or continue on a minor path on its eastern side, in which case the wall must be crossed at a slight breach when a clear trail comes into view on the western side (Wp.12 115M), as the eastern side ends at a quarry.

Descending to the clear trail

The clear trail crosses a grassy rise, bringing **Windermere** into view, then curls round the southern side of the quarry to a junction (Wp.13 124M) where we can take either path (the right hand branch is drier) down to a bright green gate (Wp.14 128M), which we cross with the help of a couple of metal steps.

We now descend towards **Baysbrown Farm** before turning right on an old quarry track (Wp.15 137M) leading into **Baysbrown Wood**. Crossing a tarmac lane (Wp.16 158M), we follow a bridleway track through a working quarry, where there's an information panel about the local slate industry. Shortly after the information panel, we bear left on a footpath (Wp.17) down to **Great Langdale Beck**, which we cross via a footbridge (Wp.18 166M) to join the road just beside **Wainwright's Inn**. After however long it takes to negotiate this welcome obstacle, we take the signposted footpath just north of the pub (Wp.19 168M) back to the **Baysbrown** farm track and the start of the walk.

Crinkle Crags is the collective name for a line of six linked summits at the western end of **Great Langdale.** Justifiably famous (and popular), they rise above **Oxendale** like an impregnable bastion, apparently impassable for all but biglegged Brobdingnagians, a discouraging impression compounded by such alarming snippets of toponymy as 'Black Wars', 'Great Knott', 'Toe Buttress', 'Great Cove', and 'Bad Step'. Inevitably, nature's dare has been gleefully taken up by mankind and the Crags are swarming with walkers of an entirely conventional stature. That's perhaps a slight exaggeration, both in terms of the challenge and the numbers accepting it, but big it is, and the fact that a good proportion of the trails are paved or in the process of being paved, suggests this is not a walk you'd want to do on a Bank Holiday weekend. On an ordinary weekday though, it's among the most thrilling and satisfying itineraries in the **Lake District**.

5   4½ H   8.1 miles/13 km   1100m / 1100m   4

Access: on foot from **Great Langdale**

> **Short Version**
> **Pike of Blisco** (see text)

We approach the crags via a slightly offbeat route over **Pike of Blisco**, a grand little peak that looks even grander on the descent along **The Band**. The Crags themselves are not manifestly dangerous, but they are a bit airy, so there's a very mild risk of vertigo. If you're using a compass, beware. Apparently an electric fence is interfering with the magnetic field, sometimes distorting it, sometimes not!

The walk starts from the National Trust 'Pay & Display' car park (£4.50 for 4h+) beside **Old Dungeon Ghyll Hotel**, passing in its first few hundred yards both the terminus of the bus from **Ambleside** (see Appendices for details) and the **Great Langdale** Campsite. If you're staying at the **New Dungeon Ghyll Hotel**, follow the **Cumbria Way** or the 'main' road to the start.

From the car park entrance (Wp.1 0M), we walk back to the B5343 and turn right to follow the **Blea Tarn** road, passing the bus stop, the **Stool End** farm drive (our return route), and a gate at the western end of the campsite (Wp.2 4M). Climbing steadily along the road, we see ahead of us the distinct declivity of **Redacre Gill**, which is lined in its lower reaches with conifer-dominated woodland.

Crinkle Crags from the road

Halfway through an S-bend (Wp.3 14M), we leave the road, contouring across a hillside on our right and passing an upright slate set in the ground, which acts as a waypost to a clear stony trail that begins a little way above the S-bend.

The trail, the first of several intermittently paved ways en route, climbs steadily (SW) crossing three affluents of **Redacre Gill**. After the third affluent (Wp.4 34M), the gradient steepens, though not as dramatically as it appears from below, and the climb is simplified by tailored steps, which make for a slow but relatively painless ascent to a couple of cairns on a pass at the head of the affluent, within sight of **Pike of Blisco** and **Bowfell** (Wp.5 62M).

Continuing on a clear trail, we traverse rough but relatively level ground before climbing to cross a tiny crag (Wp.6 77M), a hands-on job but no obstacle.

Band & Bowfell from Pike of Blisco

Cairns then guide us along a slightly less evident trail through a second hands-on scramble (Wp.7 82M). A third hands-on comes just short of the twin **Pike of Blisco** peaks, the northernmost of which (Wp.8 92M) is only visible in the last fifty yards. From here, we can see the continuation of our route, a clear path climbing from **Red Tarn** to **Great Knott**.

From the dip just south of the northern top, we follow a natural way down, initially SSW toward the **Coniston** fells then veering WSW on an increasingly clear trail to the northern end of **Red Tarn**, where we pass a path on the left to **Wrynose Pass** and another 20 yards later descending on the right to **Oxendale** (Wp.9 105M). Though steep, the **Oxendale** path is clear and straightforward, and could be used either as an escape route or to turn the present itinerary into a shorter walk.

For the full walk, we cross **Browney Gill** and follow an eroded partially tailored path, climbing steadily then gently then steadily again (WNW) to pass behind the bulbous rise of **Great Knott**. The trail briefly levels off between two cairns southwest of **Great Knott**, from where we can clearly distinguish five of the six Crags backed by the looming rise of **Bowfell** (Wp.10 125M). Continuing along the clear trail, we climb onto the end of the first crag (Wp.11 139M).

Following a clear way marked with cairns, we climb through the rocks, crossing a mini-col and a little plateau (Wp.12 146M), midway along which the path curves left and descends onto a long col above the cliffs of **Great Cove**. At the end of the col (Wp.13 151M), we have a choice of routes.

Bad Step

The main route, the so called 'Bad Step' continues directly ahead up a shallow gully, skirting to the right of a large chock-stone clearly visible above us. In all honesty, the 'Bad Step' isn't particularly bad, but if you don't like the look of it (it is a little daunting from below), bear left and take the cairn-marked route round the western side of the crag, following an obvious debris strewn path that climbs steeply to a grassy rise (Wp.14 161M), where **Bowfell** comes back into view and we see the **Scafells** for the first time.

Turning sharp right (ESE), we rejoin the principal cairn-marked trail traversing the next crag (Wp.15 171M), which we descend via a slew of boulders dotted with more cairns. We then follow a largely clear trail marked by cairns on its more obscure stretches across the final raggedy crag before descending to **Three Tarns** pass (Wp.16 192M).

Bearing right, we descend (E) onto a broad partially paved trail along the back of the wide spur known as **The Band**, passing some 550 yards later a couple of cairns (Wp.17 205M) above a junction with a faint path doubling back toward **Bowfell**.

Pike of Blisco from The Band

Continuing on the main trail (ESE), we descend along the southern flank of **The Band**, onto a second partially paved stretch (Wp.18 230M). A steady to steep descent on a winding trail leads through a kissing gate (Wp.19 249M) and then down to a track behind **Stool End Farm** (Wp.20 254M). Turning left, we follow the signposted path through the farmyard then continue along the access lane back to the start.

17 A GREAT GREAT LANGDALE ROUND:
Harrison Stickle, High Raise, Angle Tarn, Esk Pike, Bowfell, and Oxendale

Why so 'great'? A question of scale, really. First, this is our longest high mountain walk, second it encompasses two of the park's most famous peaks, **Harrison Stickle** and **Bowfell**, and third there's something intoxicating about these grand grassy uplands that inspires a sensation of expansion, as if the walker is growing bigger to fit the available space, taking giant steps in a world that's just a little bit larger than usual. Pure pleasure on a clear day, but best avoided when visibility is poor. A wide open readily legible landscape makes for easy pathfinding, despite several long sections where paths are barely discernible, but it would be easy to go astray in bad weather.

For a private plunge pool on a hot day, the stroll cannot be bettered. Take the **Stool End Farm** driveway (signposted 'Oxendale/The Band'), cross the farm yard, then follow the farm track all the way to its end, ignoring the footbridge onto the **Red Tarn** path. At the end of the track, take either of the paths along the stream then cross the footbridge at Wp.38. Bear right and go as far as heat and the urge to indulge in a grand sensory experience allow.

| 5 | 6½ H | 12.7 miles/20km | ∧ | ↗1350m ↘1350m | ⚠ | ↻ 🍴🍽 4 |

Access: on foot from Great Langdale	**Stroll**
	Hell Gill in reverse (see text and introductory notes)
	Short Versions
	Various possibilities (see text)

We start from the National Trust car park beside **Old Dungeon Ghyll Hotel** (see Walk 16 for details), but the route can easily be joined from **New Dungeon Ghyll Hotel** and the slightly cheaper car parks there by following the hotel access lane and going through the gate behind **Sticklebarn Tavern**.

From the National Trust car park (Wp.1 0M), we follow the service lane behind the hotel and go through a kissing gate, immediately veering right to go through a second kissing gate (Wp.2 2M) onto the eastbound path of the **Cumbria Way**. After two farm gateways (the second probably open), we emerge on open fell behind the new hotel (Wp.3 14M). Bearing left, we contour across the hillside to join the main paved trail alongside **Stickle Ghyll**, shortly before it reaches a footbridge (Wp.4 20M).

Ignoring the bridge, we stay on the right bank of the ghyll. After crossing a stile, we continue along the ghyll, traversing a roughly paved stretch before climbing steeply away from the main watercourse to cross an affluent (Wp.5 40M), beyond which the clear path peters out in marshy ground. Tracing a small arc doubling back to the left, we climb SSW to join a faint trodden way (visible from below) (Wp.6 46M) onto the back of **Pike Howe** (Wp.7 51M), a diminutive but dramatic little crag from where we already enjoy superb views to the south. We can also see (to the north) three of the big pikes, **Loft Crag**, **Harrison Stickle** and **Pavey Ark** though the last isn't always counted as one of the **Langdale Pikes**.

Heading north-west, we join a clear trail that climbs round the southwestern side of **Pike Howe**. For a short walk you might follow this trail back to **Stickle Ghyll** (Wp.4) or the **Cumbria Way** (Wp.3).

Loft Crag & Harrison Stickle

Otherwise, we climb steadily along the main trail, crossing a shoulder of **Harrison Stickle** and bringing the sugarloaf cone of **Pike of Stickle** into view as we pass a large pile of stones (Wp.8 73M). Following an obvious but occasionally mildly vertiginous way, we traverse the crags on the left flank of **Harrison Stickle**, until we come to a crossroads of paths at the head of **Dungeon Ghyll** (Wp.9 80M).

Peakbaggers may care to branch off here onto the well-trodden paths visiting **Loft Crag** and **Pike of Stickle**. For the present itinerary though, we turn right (NE) and follow the faintest of the branches, climbing past cairns to join a clear, partially paved way running up from the **Pike of Stickle** path.

This trail disappears momentarily, but after a brief clamber over rocks, we recover a clear way onto the summit of **Harrison Stickle** (Wp.10 92M) from where, on a clear day, you can see...well, just about everything really. Most pertinently for us, we can make out the grassy ridge separating **Mickleden** from **Langstrath**, along which we climb to **Angle Tarn** (unseen) and the clear path to the foot of **Allen Crags**. **Bowfell** is the highest summit on the ridge to the west.

Stickle Tarn from Harrison Stickle

From **Harrison Stickle**, we pick our way across the rocks (NNW), then head north across pasture to cross the scattered band of rock defining **Thunacar Knott** (Wp.11 103M), from where a trodden way leads onto the prosaically named (it's self-evidently what it says it is) **High Raise**, where there's a large windbreak and a trig point (Wp.12 127M). The summit itself is bland, but the views justify the detour.

From **High Raise**, we double back to the left (SW), aiming for **Bowfell**. Our next objective is the small tarn on **Stake Pass**, which is easily distinguishable if visibility is good - if it isn't good, you shouldn't really be up here! The descent to **Stake Pass** should be considered off-path, though we do soon find ourselves following a faint trodden way, which becomes clear as it crosses a first small torrent set in a distinct declivity (Wp.13 137M). Another clear patch appears at a second torrent, after which the faint way descends

Angle Tarn

alongside
a third,
double-sourced
watercourse for
100 yards before
crossing onto its left
bank just below an affluent
(Wp.14 147M). We continue
descending into the swale behind
Stake Pass, crossing **Stake Beck**
behind a small pebble beach (Wp.15
156M).

We then climb south-west, to join the **Cumbria Way** (Wp.16 159M), 275
yards north of a staggered crossroads on **Stake Pass** (Wp.17 166M).

The path to the left climbs to **Pike of Stickle**, while the **Cumbria Way**
continues straight ahead into **Mickleden** another option for a short version.
We, however, turn right, passing to the south of the tarn on land so
waterlogged we walk on stepping stones for the first 350 yards before
reaching a dry path (Wp.18 172M), though there are intermittent stepping
stone passages thereafter.

Following a gentle climb (SW), we pass to the right of a small outcrop of rock
at the far end of a rough plateau (Wp.19 190M). Continuing on any one of a
number of faint parallel ways (choice depends on where the ground is least
wet), we pass behind the head of a watershed, **Little Gill** (Wp.20 197M),
marked by a small cairn but I suspect too precipitous to be considered as an
optional descent. Sticking with an intermittent path (SSW), we aim for **Ore
Gap**, the col between **Esk Pike** and **Bowfell**, joining a stretch of clear path
(Wp.21 207M) shortly before coming into sight of **Angle Tarn**. After a final
traverse, we join a major trail a little way above the tarn (Wp.22 216M).

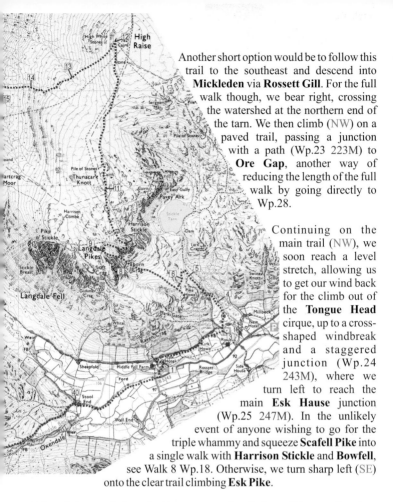

Another short option would be to follow this trail to the southeast and descend into **Mickleden** via **Rossett Gill**. For the full walk though, we bear right, crossing the watershed at the northern end of the tarn. We then climb (NW) on a paved trail, passing a junction with a path (Wp.23 223M) to **Ore Gap**, another way of reducing the length of the full walk by going directly to Wp.28.

Continuing on the main trail (NW), we soon reach a level stretch, allowing us to get our wind back for the climb out of the **Tongue Head** cirque, up to a cross-shaped windbreak and a staggered junction (Wp.24 243M), where we turn left to reach the main **Esk Hause** junction (Wp.25 247M). In the unlikely event of anyone wishing to go for the triple whammy and squeeze **Scafell Pike** into a single walk with **Harrison Stickle** and **Bowfell**, see Walk 8 Wp.18. Otherwise, we turn sharp left (SE) onto the clear trail climbing **Esk Pike**.

Although frequently breached by outcrops of rock, the trail is never less than obvious as we make our way up to a broad sheet of rock (Wp.26) 200 yards short of the summit. After traversing a debris spattered plateau, we clamber up a shallow raked boulder chute onto the top of **Esk Pike** (Wp.27 265M), from where we can see the surprisingly gentle path climbing the back of **Bowfell**. Following cairns, we descend to **Ore Gap**, where we pass the head of the alternative path from **Angle Tarn** (Wp.28 277M).

More cairns guide us across a field of boulders (ESE) onto the path we saw from **Esk Pike** (Wp.29 282M), which follows a more southerly trajectory. Though not as obvious on the ground as it appeared from above, the path is easy to follow until it peters out for the final pathless, cairn-peppered ascent across rocks onto the summit of **Bowfell** (Wp.30 298M), the southern side of which is somewhat less gentle.

We can either descend directly onto the main path on the eastern flank of the summit or, if that's busy with ascending walkers, which it often is, follow cairns across the rocks ahead (ESE) (some care required as this is limb twisting territory) down to the southern edge of the summit (Wp.31 304M).

Still following the cairns we bear left, aiming for the **Langdale Pikes** (E). At the junction with the main path (Wp.32 306M), we turn right and descend steeply on a broad but badly eroded trail to **Three Tarns Pass**.

The simplest way down from the pass is to follow the main trail along the **Band**, as detailed in Walk 16. Nonetheless, if you feel up to a little more time on obscure grassy ways, I strongly recommend the alternative route via **Oxendale**. 50 yards east of the pass we fork right (Wp.33 321M) and descend alongside the right bank of **Buscoe Sike**, following an eroded way interleaved with tailored runoff channels.

After a steep descent, the gradient eases and the erosion diminishes before disappearing altogether (Wp.34 330M). Continuing on a faint grassy way running parallel to the **Sike** (SE), we aim for **Pike of Blisco**, crossing the remnants of an ancient pen (a circle of post stumps and partially interred wire). Passing a distinct, singular crag (Wp.35 336M), probably on the right depending on how wet the ground is, we join a clearer path descending toward an obvious deepening in the course of the **Sike**.

Buscoe Sike

The path runs in tandem with the 'deepening', a spectacular mini-gorge known as **Hell Gill**, toward the end of which it becomes a paved way (Wp.36 342M) descending very steeply to the **Sike's** confluence with an affluent source (Wp.37 347M), where we pass the first in a series of perfect plunge pools. On a hot day, come prepared.

Crossing the **Sike** twice so that we stay on its right bank, we descend past increasingly tempting pools, then contour across a hillside on an eroded path high above the plunging watercourse. After skirting the head of an erosion gully, we descend on a second paved stretch and a tapering grassy slope to a footbridge (Wp.38 360M). We cross the footbridge (last chance for a bathe!) and follow the path down to the end of the **Stool End** farm track (Wp.39 365M).

We now simply follow this track, which is marked with yellow footpath arrows, all the way to the farm (Wp.40 378M). Taking the signposted footpath through the farmyard, we end the walk with a gentle stroll down the farm driveway.

Realizing previous generations had done the **Lake District** few favours by planting conifers all over the place, the Forestry Commission have sought to make amends by turning **Grizedale Forest** into a sort of sylvan theme park, patterned with nature trails and decorated with sculptures inspired by the materials to hand. This potentially ghastly idea has been a great success, largely because the installations are sufficiently striking to carry off the conceit, but also because enough broadleaf trees remain to counter the lugubrious impact of the pine.

Doubtless dedicated wilderness enthusiasts will regard this itinerary with dismay, but everyone else should have a whale of a time. Apart from one optional 20-yard off-path shortcut, it's all easy strolling on broad trails and forest tracks - toward the end we even follow an asphalted pavement! The discrete wayposted itineraries partially exploited in our walk are outlined in a leaflet available at **Coniston Information Centre** (£2.95). The end of the walk, which is the best bit for children, can be done as a stroll from the **Bogle Crag** (see Wp.20) or **Grizedale Hall** car parks, the latter also feasible with pushchairs and wheelchairs.

Access: by car, or bus from **Coniston**, **Bowness Ferry House**, and **Ulverston**.

| **Alternative Walks/Strolls** |
| See introductory notes and text |

The route begins (Wp.1)

Starting from the **Millwood** car park (£2 for 4 hours) at the northern end of **Grizedale**, we take the yellow wayposted 'Millwood Trail', which begins beside the giant lumberjack at the entrance to the car park (Wp.1 0M). Strolling through the woods below the treetop paraphernalia of the 'Go Ape' adventure park, we bear left at the 'Kennels Road' car park/picnic area (4M), then left again 50 yards later.

N.B. GPS reception is poor in these woods, but high-tech navigational gear may look a little OTT on this family friendly waymarked walk!

Sticking with the yellow route, we go straight ahead at a crossroads (Wp.2 11M) and climb steadily to join a dirt track (Wp.3 15M). Turning left, we follow the track for 275 yards, passing a first sculpture. At a second, 'fingerpost' sculpture, we turn right (Wp.4 20M) on a spur path climbing to a hungry hedgehog (see picture on next page).

We can either return to the track and take the next major turning on the right, or (as mapped) squeeze under a fallen tree behind the hedgehog and cross 20

yards of scrubland onto a broad trail (Wp.5 23M), where we turn right. Either way, we follow this trail (NW), now on the green and red routes, initially crossing a tract of closely packed re-plantation, then traversing deforested land within sight of the **Coniston Fells**.

After passing a memorial bench, we turn left at a T-junction (Wp.6 34M), and follow a track skirting more mature pine toward **Carron Crag**, the diminutive rise visible above the tops of the trees.

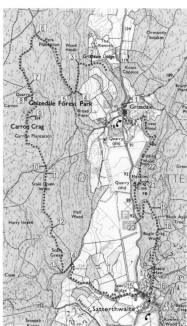

Ignoring a minor track branching right (Wp.7 42M), we bear right 75 yards later, crossing a stile onto a footpath (Wp.8 43M), which leads up to the trig point on **Carron Crag** (Wp.9 48M), from where we can see most of the high fells in the southern **Lake District**.

Continuing on the waypos ted path, we descend (S), turning right when we rejoin the dirt track (Wp.10) then going straight ahead at the crossroads 45 yards later (Wp.11), following the green route along a broad forestry track. After 450 yards, the track ends in a turning circle (Wp.12 63M) and we continue on a narrow path winding into more varied woodland (N.B. a new path is currently being laid at this point, so the next 500 yards may appear marginally different post-publication).

Insect Archway

Descending through an 'insect' archway, we cross the new path and pass an innovative bench. Emerging at a Y-junction of tracks (Wp.13 72M), we turn sharp left, doubling back on the main track then turn sharp right 100 yards later (Wp.14) on a farm track descending to **Satterthwaite** (if refreshment

is required **The Eagle's Head** is a couple of hundred yards down the road). Turning right on the main road then immediately left (Wp.15 84M), we climb a tarmac lane, passing entrances to **Pepper House B&B** and the village graveyard. At the end of the lane we take the footpath forking left (not the 'High Dale' bridleway, which is in any case due to be suppressed) (Wp.16 89M).

Forking left again at another junction 100 yards later (Wp.17), we follow the lilac wayposted footpath. At a second junction where a branch of the lilac route climbs to the right, we continue straight ahead for **Bogle Crag** car park (Wp.18 96M). Joining a track (Wp.19), we turn left and descend to the car park, an alternative starting point where parking is free.

From the car park, we take a footpath signposted 'Visitors Centre' (Wp.20 105M). The path initially runs in tandem with the road then climbs behind an old quarry to a junction (Wp.21 110M). Turning left, still for the 'Visitors Centre', we join the white itinerary, which descends to a junction of asphalted paths (Wp.22 112M), where we fork left on the white and blue routes.

If you're walking with children whose energies are beginning to flag, just watch them come alive here. So far we have seen intermittent installations (not all of them mentioned in the text), but the remainder of the walk offers constant surprises with hanging spiders, giant flies, carved sheep, stone Wendy houses, reindeer on a roof, and a series of wonderfully imaginative wooden instruments that should have the whole family banging away like a convention of percussionists.

We now simply follow the asphalted path (though children will probably be darting off all over the place and families can add a good half hour to the total time), eventually crossing the 'Grizedale Hall' car park to join the road just short of the start.

19 THE CUMBRIA WAY: LOWICK BRIDGE to CONISTON

The **Cumbria Way**, which crosses the **Lake District** from North to South, is a remarkably self-effacing piece of work, systematically shying away from all the most dramatic bits and so unassuming it rarely differentiates itself from other rights of way by distinct waymarking. As an LDP done in its entirety, I suspect it might be a little disappointing, but as a basis for easy day walks, it's ideal.

Access: by bus

> **Strolls**
> **Coniston Water**

The purpose of this itinerary is to illustrate how the **Lake District's** excellent public transport network can be exploited for linear excursions in outlying areas. Such walks will never gain the fame of their more eminent mountain cousins, nor will they satisfy those intent on 'getting to the top', or the challengers who wish to test themselves with some rare feat of endurance, but they're none the worse for that! If you want fresh air, fine views and easy walking through lovely countryside set against the backdrop of beautiful mountains, bussing out, walking back will provide the makings of a perfect day.

In this instance, we use the **X12 Ulverston** to **Coniston** service, which leaves **Coniston** from the **Crown Hotel**. We get off at **Lowick Bridge** (signposted 'Lowick' on the road) 20 minutes later. Buses leave **Coniston** at 07.50, 08.40, 10.10, 12.05, 13.35, 15.20, 16.50, and 18.10. If you're arriving by car, it might be better to park at **Lowick Bridge** and get the bus back at the end of the day. If you prefer to leave your car in **Coniston**, the John Ruskin Technology College on **Lake Road** doubles as a car park at weekends and in school holidays (£2 in the honesty box).

The first part of the walk is a pathless tramp on rights of way traversing fields that might be impassably muddy after wet weather, in which case stay on the **Lowick** road past the church and **Lowick Hall**, then turn right and follow the lane past **Park Wood** to join the described walk at Wp.9.

For the strolls, take the **Coniston Launch** (Southern route) from the end of **Lake Road** and get off at the **Sunny Bank** (Wp.26) or **Torver** (Wp.23) landings. The lakeside path passes numerous beaches, so if you want a dip in Summer, come prepared.

From the **Red Lion** bus shelter at **Lowick Bridge** (Wp.1 0M), we walk up the lane past the pub and take the right of way forking right for 'Everard Lodge' 75 yards later (Wp.2). Cutting across pathless fields (W), we cross slate steps in a wall then bear right, away from the farm buildings of **Everard Lodge**, and go through a metal gate waymarked with a yellow footpath arrow (Wp.3 8M).

Guided by the curve of the next field, we reach another stone stile (Wp.4 11M), beyond which we ford a shallow brook and follow a faint, muddy track pocked by cow hooves, bisecting a clearer track 50 yards later. Continuing off-path, we skirt the southern side of **Heads Wood** (WNW), which is in fact no more than a small rise spotted with a few scattered trees. Passing between two hummocks on the western side of the 'wood', we descend onto a faint way approaching a wire fence (Wp.5 24M) not strictly on the right-of-way, but this is the narrowest crossing over the marshy area of **Tuto Moss**. We follow the fence to the right for 125 yards, then cross another stone stile (Wp.6) and head for **Lin Crag Farm**, the white buildings visible to the northwest. After going through a wide gate (Wp.7 32M), we join **Raisthwaite Lane** (Wp.8 34M).

It is possible to take the signposted footpath via **Lin Crag Farm**, but since this goes through the farm garden and serves no great purpose apart from avoiding a short stretch of not very onerous tarmac, we turn left. When the lane veers left, we turn right on the **Long Lane** bridleway to 'Kiln Bank' (Wp.9 36M), then right again on a bridleway behind **Kiln Bank Farm** (Wp.10 41M).

We now follow a pleasant farm track, bringing **Black Combe** into view before forking right at a waypointed junction (Wp.11 45M). The track winds across high pasture spattered with outcrops of rock, getting fainter as it curves round to a ladder-stile (Wp.12 49M). We then climb toward **Tottlebank**

Farm, initially on a grassy track then on tarmac. 50 yards before the farm we turn right on a signposted 'Public Footpath'(Wp.13 58M).

The trail initially heads east, but soon veers north and dwindles to a path, skirting **Tottlebank Heights** before descending to a staggered crossroads just short of **Cockenskell Farm**. We go through a 'Cumbria Way' gate below a solitary oak (Wp.14 71M) and follow a faint trodden way skirting a pasture before going through another gate and forking left (Wp.15 74M) down to a bridge over **Tarn Beck**.

Tarn Beck

Beyond the beck there's a maze of crisscrossing ways. Choosing in each instance the better trod way and maintaining a northerly direction, we climb steadily to cross a small rise and reach **Beacon Tarn** (Wp.16 86M).

The **Cumbria Way** goes round the western side of the tarn, but a more interesting if narrower and rougher path skirts the **Bleak Knott** shore on the right. Either way, the two routes rejoin at the northern end of the tarn to climb a small rise before skirting to the right of a marshy area, at the far end of which we pass a large pile of stones (Wp.17 104M).

Beacon Tarn

Following a clear, narrow path, we curve east to avoid the great marshy expanse of **Stable Harvey Moss**. After forking left at a Y-junction (Wp.18

110M), we clip the tip of a tarmac access lane, and turn left (Wp.19 117M) on a signposted bridleway (not the footpath alongside the wall 30 yards later).

Though both bridleway and footpath end at more or less the same place, the principle advantage of the former is that it climbs less, in keeping with which we ignore a shortcut forking right 150 yards later (Wp.20).

Torver Beck

When the track runs into a confusion of ways at the meeting of two sets of power cables, we cross **Mere Beck** (Wp.21 126M) and follow a clearly trodden way that soon bears northeast to cross an affluent. We then descend alongside **Mere Beck** to a footbridge over **Torver Beck** and climb to the A5084, where we take the signposted route for 'Coniston via Lake Shore' (Wp.22 139M).

Initially a track, this route soon dwindles to a trail descending to the **Coniston Launch Sunny Bank** landing (Wp.23 146M). From here, it's simply a matter of following your nose (north!), traversing one of the loveliest lakeside woods in the park; the birch and sessile oak are particularly splendid. You certainly won't want to be reading a book here, but for pacing progress, we go through the first of two gates after a little under a mile (Wp.24 164M) and fork right (Wp.25 168M) immediately after the second gate to stay alongside the shore.

After passing a footpath to **Torver** and the **Torver Coniston Launch** landing (Wp.26 174M), we reach a broad trail leading into a less agreeable stretch of shore overrun by campsites. Staying as close to the shore as we can, we pass the **Park Coppice** campsite and go into the **Coniston Hall** site. Eventually, at a water-speed limit 30 yards from a wall (Wp.27 192M), we are obliged to bear left and follow the campsite track up to **Coniston Hall**, unmistakable with its four massive chimneys. 100 yards up the **Haws Bank** road (Wp.28 199M), we turn right on a very broad trail, which we follow across flat pasture to emerge on **Lake Road** (Wp.29 212M), 375 yards from the junction with the A593 (Wp.30), 275 yards from the **Coniston Launch** car park if you're doing the stroll.

Other suggestions for linear walks using public transport:
> **Grasmere** to **Ambleside** via **Loughrigg Terrace** and **Rydall Hall**
> **Great Langdale** to **Skelwith Bridge** (**Cumbria Way**)
> **Skelwith Bridge** to **Coniston** (**Cumbria Way**)
> **Kendal** to **Bowness** or **Windermere** (**Dales Way**)
> **Kentmere** to **Staveley** via **Ullthwaite Bridge** and **Park House**

A delightful lakeside stroll, fabulous forests both benign and menacing, and superb views of lofty heights, all conspire to make this the Bonaparte of low level walks; short but goes everywhere and achieves stature by its ceaseless twists and turns.

The National Trust owns about four fifths of the Lake District and, like many walks, this itinerary is almost entirely on trust land. In this instance the woodland is particularly rich, including sessile oak, birch, rowan, hazel, ash, wych elm, and bird cherry. One of the Trust's earliest benefactors was Near Sawrey resident Mrs. William Heelis, better known as Beatrix Potter. **The Tower Bank Arms** in **Near Sawrey** features in The Tale of Jemima Puddleduck while **Esthwaite Water** inspired The Tale of Jeremy Fisher.

*Nothing en route. Nearest refreshments are in **Far Sawrey** (see Wp.8), **Outgate**, **Hawkshead**, and **Near Sawrey**.

Access: by car or ferry from **Bowness** or (summer service) bus from **Hawkshead**.

Stroll
Along the shores of the lake, north or south.

To reach the start, take the B5285/B5286 between **Coniston**, **Hawkshead** and **Ambleside**, then make your way to **High Wray**, either via 'Hawkshead' or 'Low Wray'. In **High Wray**, take the narrow lane signposted 'Ferry 3 unfit for vehicles after 1 mile'. Follow the lane down to the lakeside and park in the free **Red Nab** car park. The walk can be joined from the **Bowness Ferry** stage (accessible by bus from **Hawkshead** in the summer) by following the lane north to Wp.5, or taking the 'White Post' route directly to Wp.7.

The Lakeside Track

From the car park (Wp.1 0M), we stroll along the **Belle Grange** driveway, staying on the lakeside track as it passes a signposted junction with a bridleway climbing directly to **Latterbarrow** (Wp.2 6M). A lovely stroll amid trees so august they confirm the imperial conceit of the introduction, takes us past a track doubling back to the right and (a kindly but faintly superfluous appendage) a 'Wildlife Viewing Platform' (Wp.3 19M).

We continue along the lakeside track under an abstract of red, brown and green broadleaves, set amid scattered clusters of bracken and rocks wrapped in moss. Ignoring a branch descending to the left (Wp.4 24M), we skirt behind the **Strawberry Gardens** trailer park, forking right 550 yards later on the **Far Sawrey** bridleway (Wp.5 31M).

Far Sawrey bridleway

Climbing steadily, we carry straight on at a staggered crossroads (Wp.6 43M) to continue our ascent (SW). After a gate, we come to a junction with a path climbing from the ferry (Wp.7 51M). We now follow the 'White Post' route all the way to **Latterbarrow**, so except for the unmarked

Waypoint 8

junction at Wp.9, the book can safely be put away for the next ninety odd minutes. All other junctions are sign or wayposted. We continue along the **Far Sawrey** bridleway for another 300 yards, then turn right (Wp.8 55M) on a track climbing a rise, briefly bringing into view the **Coniston Fells**, **Crinkle Crags**, and **Bowfell**.

Forking right at a Y-junction (Wp.9 64M), we descend slightly, the track dwindling to a path, then climb to a junction (White Post No.4), where we turn left (W) for 'Hawkshead' (Wp.10 74M).

Our trail winds between tall tenebrous pine, so spindly they sway back and forth in the breeze like a band of inebriates propping up the bar at last orders and, as with the inebriates, one among the merry band occasionally loses its footing and topples over, so beware in a high wind. There's no path here and some care is required to follow the wayposts which guide us through the woods in the manner of some fairytale confection contrived for Hansel and Gretel. The suggestion of an enchanted landscape continues on the heights of **High Pate Crag**, where we turn right, as indicated by a fingerpost at the far end of 10-foot high ridge of rock protruding from the ground like the back of a slumbering beast (Wp.11 80M).

We immediately dip back into the woodland (NW), swinging round to cross a footbridge (Wp.12 83M) shortly before a signposted junction doubles back on the right to a 'View point' on **High Blind How** (Wp.13 90M). Returning to the main path, we descend (NE), turning left at a T-junction (Wp.14 92M) to join a dirt track. Turning right then left 50 yards later (White Post No.6; Wp.15 95M), we follow a path skirting the breezy, rather scruffy re-plantation of **Claife Heights**, where we have fine views of the **Fairfield Horseshoe** and **Langdale Pikes**.

We then curve round to a signposted junction just above the dirt track (Wp.16 105M), where we turn left, once again burrowing into more mature, more lugubrious woodland, in which the white-tipped wayposts are vital. Running into the bend of another track (Wp.17 110M), we maintain direction (NW), passing a crossroads with a path 50 yards later. At the next crossroads (White Post No.10; Wp.18 116M), we have a choice of routes. To cut short the main walk, turn right on the bridleway descending to 'Belle Grange' and the start of the walk. For the full walk, we take the 'Hawkshead' trail doubling back on the left to a signposted junction, where we bear right for 'Latterbarrow' (Wp.19 119M).

Dipping down to cross a swathe of devastated woodland (it looks like a giant's been playing skittles), we follow a complicated but well wayposted route coiling through the woods. After negotiating more twists and turns than a political thriller, we cross a stile (Wp.20) and fork right for the final 275 yards on a broad trail climbing across the bracken-backed **Latterbarrow** to its high point (Wp.21 138M), where we are rewarded with views of nearly all the southern Lakes' high mountains.

Heading north-east towards **Wansfell**, just south of **Ambleside**, we descend to a kissing gate (Wp.22 143M) and a Y-junction of tracks below the National Trust volunteers 'Base Camp' (Wp.23 150M). We follow the main access track down to the road through **High Wray**. Strolling through the village, we pass the lane we took to reach the car park, and turn right 45 yards after the postbox and village hall, on a right of way signposted 'To Lake' (Wp.24 163M). After skirting three fields, we reach the shore (Wp.25 170M) and turn right to return to the start.

21 LITTLE LANGDALE via TILBERTHWAITE & HOLME FELL

Old mines, abandoned quarries, bubbling brooks, a positively alpine pasture, fine forests, a modest fell cradling an immoderately evocative tarn, plus a country pub and a tea shop, both perfectly placed to serve their respective functions, make this an excellent low level walk. It goes up and down a bit, especially toward the end, so the full circuit isn't really suitable for families with small children, but otherwise it should be well within the capabilities of every averagely energetic walker.

	Strolls
	(a) Miners Bridge (see text)
Access: on	**(b) Tilberthwaite** to **Little Langdale** (see Walk 21 for access)
foot from	**(c) Holme Fell** from **Little Langdale**
Coniston	**(d) Holme Fell** from **Glen Mary** car park, 100 metres east of Wp.26 on the A593
	(e) Tarn Hows Cottage (see text)

We start from the **John Ruskin Technology College** on **Lake Road** (Wp.1 0M), which serves as a car park at weekends and during school holidays (£2 in the honesty box, please). If you're starting from elsewhere, join the walk at the junction on the A593 just south of the BP station. From the college, we walk up to the A593 and continue straight ahead on **Station Road**, then dip down to the signposted 'Footpath' beside **The Sun Inn** (Wp.2 4M).

Miner's Bridge

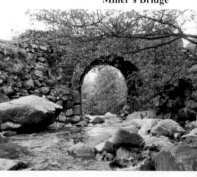

Behind **Dixon Ground Farm**, we follow a track across a field, crossing **Scrow Beck** before climbing alongside the racing torrent of **Church Beck** to **Miner's Bridge** (Wp.3 17M). For a stroll, cross the bridge and take the main track back to **Coniston**, or continue upstream to explore (cautiously) the mine workings around the youth hostel before retracing your steps. For the full walk, we cross the bridge and follow the main track upstream, forking right 150 yards later (Wp.4).

We bear right at the next two junctions (Wp.5 & 6), then turn left at the third junction (Wp.7 27M). After a long, steady northerly climb, we pass a stretch of anti-erosion fencing and a minor path forking left toward **Wetherlam** (Wp.8 48M). Staying on the main trail, we maintain a northeasterly direction across a long level pass before descending alongside **Crook Beck** into the attractive, quasi-alpine landscape above **Tilberthwaite**.

After crossing an affluent (Wp.9 65M), our trail descends to the head of **Tilberthwaite Gill** and a junction with a branch from the main **Birk Fell** trail

(Wp.10 76M). Bearing right, we stroll along a lovely path high above **Tilberthwaite Gill**, skirting one or two slightly precipitous slopes before descending past **Tilberthwaite Quarry** to a car park (Wp.11 88M).

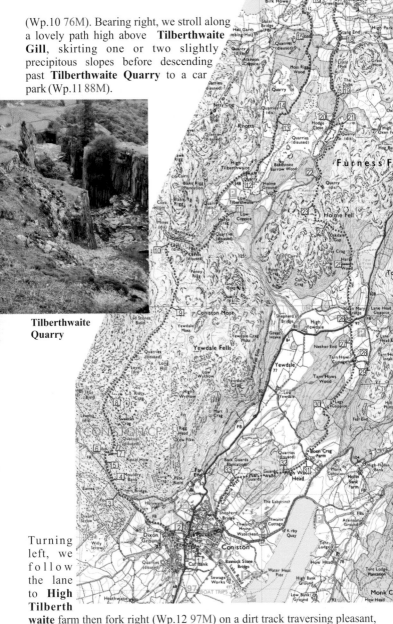

Tilberthwaite Quarry

Turning left, we follow the lane to **High Tilberthwaite** farm then fork right (Wp.12 97M) on a dirt track traversing pleasant, peaceful countryside dotted with partially overgrown piles of quarry spoil. Staying on the main track, we ignore all branches, including a major fork on the left (Wp.13 107M) and a major branch doubling back on the right (Wp.14 109M), until we come to a signposted junction (Wp.15 120M), where we have a choice of routes. If you don't want to go to the pub (Que?) turn right for 'Colwith/Skelwith', rejoining the described route at Wp.18. Otherwise, turn left for 'Hallgarth', crossing a footbridge and following a lane up to the **Wrynose** road (Wp.16 129M), where we turn right to reach **The Three**

Shires Inn.

Continuing along the lane after the pub, we pass **Wilson Place Farm** then turn right on a signposted 'Footpath' (Wp.17 133M), re-crossing the stream via a footbridge and climbing back to the **Colwith/Skelwith** lane. Crossing the lane, we maintain direction (S) on a track for 'Hodge Close' (Wp.18 141M). At a junction with a path to 'High Park' (Wp.19 151M), we bear right, staying on the track until it runs into the end of **Hodge Close** lane beside a house called **Wythe Howe** (Wp.20 154M). Forking left, we follow another track for 75 yards, then turn right on a footpath signposted 'Holm Ground/Yewdale' (Wp.21), which curves round **Parrod Quarry**.

... an exquisite reservoir ...

After passing a stile in the fence on our right, we go through a gate then turn left at a junction (Wp.22 172M). A steady climb (bear this in mind if you're stopping at the pub) leads to an exquisite reservoir on the **High Ground** of **Holme Fell**. Happily (I'm taking the pub as given here), we don't climb to the very top of the fell, but skirt to the right of the reservoir then bear left (Wp.23 179M), following one among several faint marshy ways up to a grassy pass between the main crags.

At a crossroads marked by a large pile of stones (Wp.24 184M), we maintain direction (SE) on a cairn marked path descending quite steeply into **Harry Guards Woods**. We follow the clear path as it curves south, then turn right at a slanting T-junction (Wp.25 195M), after which wayposts guide us down to the A593 and the **Yew Tree Farm Tea Rooms** (Wp.26 203M). On the far side of the road, we take the right-of-way signposted 'Tarn Hows Cottage 500 yards'. There's no path, but wayposts mark the way (S) up to a stile below a splendid oak (Wp.27 208M). Climbing to the left of the cottage, we turn right on a National Trust signposted right-of-way (Wp.28 211M), passing between the cottage and an outbuilding, and very briefly joining the **Cumbria Way**, not that you'd know it from the waymarking. Ignoring the path signposted 'Coniston/Lower Yewdale' (the **Cumbria Way** and an optional ascent for Stroll (e), returning via the described route), we take the 'Tarn Hows' route, going through a gate into a field immediately beyond the cottage (Wp.29).

Following a faint grassy track (SW), we pass to the right of the high ground in the next field then curve round to cross a stile into a third field (Wp.30 219M). Bearing left, we descend to an unsurfaced lane, where we turn left then immediately right (Wp.31 226M) for 'Guards Wood/Coniston'. After going through a gate, we fork right at a wayposted junction (Wp.32 230M), climbing over the heights of **Guards Wood** before descending to rejoin the **Cumbria Way** on a broad grassy trail (Wp.33 236M). Turning left, we descend to a stone bridge and join a slip road opposite the primary school (Wp.34 242M). Turning left again, we follow the slip road down to the B5285, where we turn right to return to our starting point through the centre of **Coniston**.

Usually visited in the context of **Old Man** loops, **Swirl How** is also the culminating point of a little frequented but near perfect horseshoe starting from **Little Langdale** or, as here, the picturesque mining hamlet of **Tilberthwaite**. It's a relatively strenuous walk and involves some off-path navigation, but is worth the effort for the superb views and the idyllic descent through the abandoned levels, mines and quarries of **Tilberthwaite**, now such a perfectly peaceful place it's hard to equate it with the industrial din that riddled these hills with holes.

5   4½ H   8.3 miles/13.4km   850m / 850m   4

Stroll
Tilberthwaite Gill and **Birk Fell** mine in reverse (see text)
The stroll is strongly recommended for those disinclined to tackle the full itinerary. **Tilberthwaite Gill** stems from two superb little waterfalls, the larch and rowan lining the gully are lovely, while the disused workings below **Birk Fell** evoke a melancholic serenity that would have had the Romantics racing to sharpen their quills.

* N e a r e s t refreshments are in **Coniston**

Access: by car. To reach the start, take the A593 north from **Coniston** and turn left on the signposted lane to 'Tilberthwaite'. Park in the large, free car park just before **Tilberthwaite Gill**.

If you're doing the stroll, go through the gate on your left at Wp.4 and follow the main trail up to Wp.32. The return can be done as described or by taking the branch path at Wp.31 to cross the head of **Tilberthwaite Gill** and follow the right bank back to the parking area (see Walk 21 Wp.10).

From the car park (Wp.1 0M), we cross **Tilberthwaite Gill** and stroll along the road for 100 yards then turn left on a signposted path climbing past a row of miners' cottages (Wp.2).

Climbing from Wp.4

Forking left at the first junction (Wp.3 5M) then right 75 yards later (Wp.4), we climb steeply (NW) parallel to a fence, then cross a stile (Wp.5 13M). After two steep climbs alongside a wall, we reach a long level stretch, at the end of which we clamber over a stile in a lateral fence (Wp.6 32M) and cross a rise, passing a ladder-stile (Wp.7) and bringing into view the **Langdale Pikes**, **Crinkle Crags**, the road descending from **Wrynose Pass**, and beyond **Greenburn Beck**, a clear path climbing onto the tip of our horseshoe below **Rough Crags**. The main path descends steeply to **Greenburn Beck** before climbing directly to **Rough Crags**, apparently working on the premise that a straight line is the best way between two points. Possessing a less linear notion of progress, sheep apply a more oblique method. We follow the sheep. It's longer, but more agreeable and less strenuous.

Bearing left, away from the wall (W), we cross a meagre watercourse and join a sheep walk curving round the mountain (Wp.8 35M). The way follows a contour toward the rocky summit of **Pike of Blisco**, then curves southwest (Wp.9 39M), bringing the western wall of **Wet Side Edge** and Hell Gill Pike into view. We descend slightly toward the abandoned mine works on **Greenburn Beck**, passing two cairns (Wp.10 44M), after which we traverse a slew of rocks onto a higher contour pricked by a solitary metal fencing post (Wp.11 50M).

Our next objective is the reservoir dyke at the head of **Greenburn Beck**. **The Way Of The Sheep** is more obscure here, but staying on the high ground to avoid the lower marshy areas, we pass the rusting remains of a couple of oil barrels (Wp.12 59M). Maintaining both height and direction (W) for 300 yards, we reach a knot of rock (Wp.13 64M) on a rise directly above the reservoir. Turning sharp right, we descend off-path on largely dry grass (some of the turf toward the bottom is a bit spongy, but not ankle-grabbingly so) to cross the dyke (Wp.14 68M).

Swirl How from Rough Crags

After fording **Greenburn Beck**, we head northeast, still off-path, skirting the marshy ground flanking the beck. We cross faint traces of a track sweeping up the valley (Wp.15) then, 100 yards later, join the clear **Rough Crags** path seen from Wp.7 (Wp.16 80M). Doubling back to the left, we climb steeply in a westerly direction to the first rise of our horseshoe, from where we see **Crinkle Crags** again (Wp.17 94M).

We now simply follow the ridge, climbing across a succession of mini-rises on unblemished grassy paths scarred only by an effusion of love concerning a certain Phil and Sally. Climbing steadily, we pass a cairn and a large pile of stones (Wp.18 114M), immediately after which a path from **Wrynose** feeds in from the right.

Swirl How

Curving round **Wet Side Edge** (SSW) on a broader trail, we fork left at a Y-junction (Wp.19 132M) and climb onto the first of the **Carrs** summits (Wp.20 142M). Continuing over the next, slightly higher summit, we enjoy a nice airy ridge walk (possibly a little too airy in a high wind) up to **Swirl How** (Wp.21 155M).

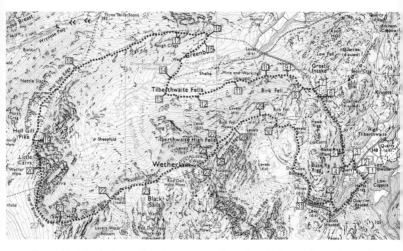

From **Swirl How**, we head east on a broad trail descending along the fragmented spine of **Prison Band** to a junction of paths on **Swirl Hawse** pass (Wp.22 180M). The path on the right descends to **Coniston**, but we continue straight ahead, climbing **Keld Gill Head** (ENE). The path levels out briefly behind **Black Sails** (Wp.23 191M), then winds along a contour, after which we traverse a fairly featureless rise before a brief, cairn-marked climb brings us onto the top of **Wetherlam**.

From the second of the cairn-capped **Wetherlam** summits (Wp.24 201M), the most obvious descents are to the south. We, however, take a less clearly defined way to the north-east, which starts directly behind the summit. Winding through rocks abraded by boots and hooves, we head for **Little Langdale Tarn**, soon bringing into view a clear trail snaking down from **Birk Fell** (Wp.25 205M). N.B. Don't worry too much about reaching precisely these waypoints, as there are two distinct trails both descending in the same direction (ENE).

Picking our way through the rocks and looking out for the cairns, we see **Birk Fell Hawse**, the col between **Wetherlam** and **Birk Fell** (Wp.26 210M). The two descents join (Wp.27 213M) amid a confusion of shortcuts, after which we zigzag down toward **Birk Fell Hawse**, which we reach via a sloping table of rock tipped with a cairn (Wp.28 221M).

We now follow an obvious and easy path along the back of the undulating ridge for 250 yards before forking right on a faint way skirting the last two rises of **Birk Fell** (Wp.29 231M) - this junction is easily missed, but as easily recovered if you find yourself on the penultimate rise.

Winding off the fell towards a patch of brown marsh, we pass a fenced sinkhole (Wp.30 236M) amid old mine workings. Following a well-tailored stairway, we descend to a broad mining trail, which curves round the hillside to the south. At a junction above the cleft of **Tilberthwaite Gill** (Wp.31 251M), we follow the main trail to the left, then turn right 225 yards later on a path topped with slate retaining steps (Wp.32 254M), descending steeply to a footbridge. We return to the car park via the path along the right bank of the Gill.

23 GRASMERE'S MENAGERIE:
The Lion, The Lamb and The Calf

Generations of tourists have been schooled to discern the lineaments of 'The Lion and The Lamb' amid the summit rocks of **Helm Crag**, and some excursionists claim entire pridefuls and flockloads are frolicking about up there, every rock an emblem of improbable harmony. As it happens, apart from some catty comments about the weather and a handful of living lambs, I encountered nothing very feline or ovine about the setup, but then I never was the sharpest walking-pole in the shop, so I'm prepared to take it on trust. And I can comfort myself with the fact that my instinctive comparison of the more northerly summit rocks to a cannon, was confirmed by the discovery that they're also dubbed 'The Howitzer'.

But whatever you see or don't see in the rocks scarcely matters, for this is a lovely little ridge, with a rugged appeal way beyond it's diminutive stature, possessing an agreeable hint of wildness without any sense of that wildness wishing to do you corporeal damage, and boasting one of the most beguiling pastoral outlooks in the **South Lakes**. The full walk is not recommended when visibility is poor as the terrain around the third component of our menagerie, **Calf Crag**, is confusing in the mist. I know I never actually got to go there when the cloud wasn't hugging my ankles!

| 3 | 3.4 H | 8.1 miles/13km | ⋀⋁ | 570m / 570m | ↻ | 3 |

Approaching the end of Easedale Road

We start on the 'Silver How' footpath along the **Allan Bank** driveway, which leaves the **Langdale Road** between **The Red Lion Hotel** and **Miller Howe Café** (Wp.1 0M). 150 yards up the drive, just after the 'Allan Bank' gateway, we turn right (Wp.2), bringing the rise of **Helm Crag** into view, and follow a wayposted path through a kissing gate (Wp.3 4M) to shadow then join the **Easedale Road**. We follow the **Easedale Road** till it ends at **Jackdaw Cottage**, where we fork right for 'Far Easedale/Helm Crag' (Wp.4 18M) on a trail climbing to a wooden gate, 25 yards after which we turn right for 'Helm Crag' (Wp.5 21M).

Turning right again at a T-junction 50 yards later (Wp.6), we zigzag up the

waypoint 5

Cannon (Howitzer)

southern side of a small quarry, passing a stretch where the path is lined with a handrail.

A steady zigzagging climb on a well paved trail is followed by a succession of gentler traverses behind the quarry, passing a fine, natural viewing point overlooking **Far Easedale** to the **Sourmilk Gill** waterfalls (Wp.7 34M). After passing a first cairn (Wp.8 39M), already within sight of the ridge, we follow a broad grassy trail cutting through banks of bracken to a triple fork (Wp.9 42M).

'Wanted - One Lion'

Any branch will do, the more southerly forks merely skirting closer to the rise overlooking **Grasmere**, all ways merging after 50 yards for a northwesterly climb onto the narrow, rocky ridge. Traversing several crags that may or may not have you reaching for your bestiary, we reach a large cairn (Wp.10 54M) behind the 'cannon', AKA The Howitzer, The Lion and The Lamb, or The Lion Couchant please pencil in your own interpretation in the space provided_____.

Following a clear stony trail marked by large cairns, we descend along the back of the ridge (NW) to the **Bracken Hause** col (Wp.11 61M). For the next three quarters of an hour, it's simply a question of keeping on keeping on along the ridge, so you may care to put the book away for this stretch. We climb to the northwest, winding between a multiplicity of mini-summits strung along **Gibson Knott**, and passing a large conical cairn (Wp.12 76M).

Following the clear path, we descend very slightly to a second col, then continue our meandering course through outcrops of rock and wannabe-summits.

Ignoring a minor path forking right (Wp.13 97M), we stay on the main trail as it climbs in a more westerly direction behind **Pike of Carrs**, where the path levels out (Wp.14 102M), then descends very slightly to cross a scar of mud. Traversing a series of muddy patches, we pass a small rise backed by a cairn (Wp.15 108M), beyond which the broadest and muddiest of the scars has to be crossed (most easily done to the left), after

Helm Crag from the North

which cairns and a trodden way lead us onto the **Calf Crag** summit, where there's a small cairn (Wp.16 116M).

50 yards to the west, another cairn (Wp.17) marks the continuation of the path, which is currently very muddy but is due to be paved, so should be easy to follow by the time of publication.

After crossing a watershed, we climb over a rocky rise then skirt to the left of a small nameless summit, beyond which we turn sharp left at a large cairn flanked by fencing posts (Wp.18 126M).

Though initially obscure, the trail into **Far Easedale** soon becomes clearer, and should, once again, be partially paved by the time of going to press. A steady, southeasterly descent leads to a ford across **Far Easedale Gill** (Wp.19 137M). We now simply follow the obvious **Far Easedale** path (SE), briefly veering away from the gill to skirt marshy, low lying ground.

After traversing rough ground littered with debris and fissured with springs, we eventually curve round the flank of a small rise overlooking a sheepfold, within sight of the **Stythwaite Steps** footbridge (Wp.20 157M). Bearing left at a junction with a wayposted path to **Easedale Tarn** (Wp.21 164M), we cross the footbridge and follow a broad trail, initially on the banks of the gill then along the wall that steers us away from the watercourse, rejoining our outward route at Wp.6 (182M).

If you feel the need to get off the beaten path, then this is the itinerary for you, featuring a central section that follows no paths whatsoever, visiting the little frequented **Tarn Crag** and **Codale Tarn** before descending onto the popular **Easedale Tarn** trail. The infrequency of visitors is attested to by the lack of paths on the top and the fact that the day I recorded this route, I saw two deer, who were clearly quite as astonished to see me as I was to see them. In view of the off-path section, the itinerary is only suitable for experienced hikers with good navigational skills. Not recommended when visibility is poor. The strolls and short version are accessible to all walkers.

Access: on foot from **Grasmere**

Strolls
(a) Far Easedale Gill (linear)
(b) Sourmilk Gill (linear)

Short Version
Easedale Tarn (see text)

We start as per Walk 23 on the 'Silver How' footpath along the **Allan Bank** driveway, which leaves the **Langdale Road** between T**he Red Lion Hotel** and **Miller Howe Café** (Wp.1 0M). 150 yards up the drive, just after the 'Allan Bank' gateway, we bear right on a waypoted path (Wp.2) crossing a field and going through a kissing gate (Wp.3 5M). The path shadows then joins the **Easedale Road**, which we follow till it ends at **Jackdaw Cottage**, where we fork right (Wp.4 18M) then left 100 yards later (Wp.5) for 'Far Easedale/Borrowdale'.

Following a broad trail along the valley, we soon see off to our left the silvery veins of the **Sourmilk Gill** waterfalls and the scar of the **Easedale Tarn** trail. After a pleasant stroll up the valley, we cross **Far Easedale Gill** via a footbridge and come to a Y-junction (Wp.6 40M). For the short version, bear left here and follow the waypoted path up to the tarn, joining the described descent at Wp.21. For the full itinerary, we fork right and continue up **Far Easedale**, climbing gently on a clear trail. The path more or less levels out between two rises, after which we cross the second of two distinct affluents (Wp.7 68M).

Entering Far Easedale Gill

Approaching the head of the valley, we pass a tailored run-off channel and a large pile of stones (Wp.8 79M). After a steady climb, the main path crosses back onto the left bank of **Far Easedale Gill** (Wp.9 82M). This is where we leave the path, staying on the right bank of the gill and bearing left, off-path, toward the steep grassy slope that forms a

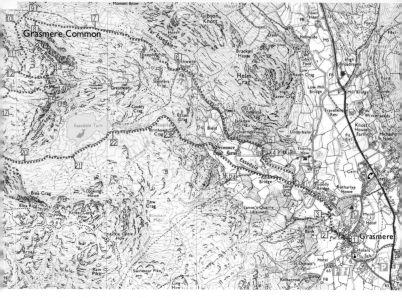

natural break in the long line of crags flanking **Far Easedale**.

Crossing an affluent gill, we circle round a grassy hummock to the foot of the steep slope (Wp.10 84M), from where the line of the affluent climbs to a V-shaped crux just below the visible horizon. This affluent, further identifiable after a few metres by a small fin-like rock, is our guiding line for the main ascent. At this point, it's more of a watershed than anything else and the turf is dry underfoot as we climb steeply (not quite as steep as it looks from below, but not recommended as a descent), crisscrossing the watershed according to convenience.

Favouring the left hand fork of the V as we near the visible top, we climb very steeply between the main watershed and a parallel watershed on our left, distinguished by a solitary oak in its bed. Zigzagging back and forth to break the incline, we pass the head of the oak-watershed (Wp.11 98M), where there's a small outcrop of rock that has a distinct conical silhouette from below. We continue climbing on rough, spongy turf, zigzagging up toward the head of the long sloping swale feeding the watersheds, until we reach a level pass and a junction of very faint trodden ways, within sight of the tip of **Codale Tarn** (Wp.12 108M).

Turning left, we follow a very faint way (E) weaving between outcrops of rock to the tiny, cairn-topped summit of **Tarn Crag** (Wp.13 115M), from where we can discern the old paths climbing from **Easedale Tarn**. Not that you'll be looking at them too closely. The view over **Grasmere** is far too good to permit of anything so mundane as picking out mere paths!

Tarn Crag

Easedale Tarn

To descend, still very much off-path, we cross the small rise south of **Tarn Crag**, on the edge of which we find a pile of stones overlooking **Easedale Tarn** (Wp.14 119M). Heading WSW, we pick up an infinitely faint sheep-trod curving below a slew of debris to a flat rock with an exceptional outlook on **Easedale Tarn** (Wp.15).

Without losing altitude, we continue in a westerly direction (off-path though the wishful eye may conjure the odd sheep-trod in the tufty grass), aiming for **Codale Tarn** when it's visible, **Harrison Stickle** and **Pavey Ark** when it's not. To avoid losing too much ground directly, we gradually curve round toward **Lang Crag** (NW), at the foot of which lies a large sheepfold. 50 yards short of the sheepfold, we join a patch of relatively clear path descending from Wp.12 (Wp.16 129M).

Turning left, we follow an intermittent, faint way down to **Codale Tarn** (Wp.17 134M). At the tarn, we bear left on a clear, narrow path between the water and **Belles Knott**, beyond which we join a major, partially paved trail descending from **Sergeant Man** (see Walk 25) on which we again turn left (Wp.18 142M).

The trail passes a shelf of rock 125 yards later (Wp.19), then zigzags down a rough route marked with regular cairns before levelling out and crossing stepping stones on marshy ground between **Easedale Tarn** and **Eagle Crag** (Wp.20 154M). After passing a solitary, moribund tree (Wp.21 153M), we stroll along the southern side of the tarn to a Y-junction (Wp.22 161M), where the short version joins the full itinerary.

Forking right, we descend along **Sourmilk Gill**, passing a spur doubling back on the left to a large plunge pool (Wp.23 173M). A straightforward descent on a broad trail brings us to a signposted crossroads (Wp.24 185M). Carrying straight on, we stroll alongside **Easedale Beck**, rejoining the **Easedale Road** 500 yards later (Wp.25).

Easedale Beck

25 STEEL FELL & SERGEANT MAN

A large loop encompassing the distinctive rise of **Steel Fell** and the grand wilderness behind the **Langdale Pikes** before descending to join the popular **Easedale Tarn** trail used in Walk 24. **Steel Fell**, which resembles a stylized reptile when seen from the road, is often neglected, partly because the land behind it is notoriously boggy, partly because the focus of attention tends to be on its more famous neighbour, **Helm Crag**. This is a pity as it's a fine little hill providing both an interesting perspective on the **Helm Crag** rocks and a novel approach to **Calf Crag**. The itinerary was recorded in driving rain and dense mist, a dedication to duty that does not merit duplication. Anyone wishing to actually enjoy themselves should leave it for a fine day. Though a 'way' of sorts is followed throughout, pathfinding without a GPS occasionally calls for a large dose of confidence laced with a dash of optimism.

We start as per Walks 23 & 24 on the 'Silver How' footpath along the **Allan Bank** driveway, which leaves the **Langdale Road** between **The Red Lion Hotel** and **Miller Howe Café** (Wp.1 0M). 150 yards up the drive, just after the 'Allan Bank' gateway, we turn right (Wp.2), and follow a wayposted path through a kissing gate (Wp.3 5M) to shadow then join the **Easedale Road**.

Waypoint 4

45 yards after the path joins the road, we turn right on a lane signposted 'Thorney How' youth hostel (Wp.4 10M). We follow this lane for half a mile until it ends at a T-junction (Wp.5 23M), where we turn left. Forking left at a Y-junction 500 yards later (Wp.6 29M), we follow a driveway up to the gated entrance to the National Trust 'Green Burn' property (Wp.7 33M).

Turning right immediately after the gate, we climb steadily on a good grassy path cutting across a bracken clad slope to a wooden gate (Wp.8 42M). Maintaining direction (NNW), we climb to a kissing-gate (Wp.9 48M), after which a narrower, rockier path skirts to the right of a first crag (Wp.10 66M).

Staying on the back of the ridge, we follow a clear, grassy path climbing in easy stages across successive rises to the debris strewn foot of the summit (Wp.11 70M). The path gets rockier again for the climb onto the top of the fell, where we meander between grassy hummocks before reaching the **Dead Pike** summit cairns, the first distinguished by a starburst of fencing posts (Wp.12 76M). The second, larger cairn 50 yards to the NW (Wp.13) marks the start of our first descent.

Following a sketchy path broken by frequent patches of bog, we descend

alongside a fence. Passing two concrete based fencing posts standing apart from the main fence (Wp.14 84M), the path briefly veers left to avoid a small drop. At the corner of the fence 100 yards later (Wp.15), we maintain a westerly direction, following a rough trail marked with more, solitary, freestanding fence posts. Favouring the trodden way when it diverges from the fencing posts, we gradually veer round to a more south-westerly direction, passing to the left of a small tarn (Wp.16 94M).

Continuing along an intermittent path, we reach an isolated pair of fencing posts standing 10 yards apart from one another (Wp.17 100M), at which point we bear left, traversing very boggy ground to recover a faint trail 200 yards later (Wp.18). This trail weaves (SSW) between peat hags, outcrops of rock, and patches of marshy ground up to **Calf Crag** summit cairn (Wp.19 114M).

Ignoring the path off to the left, which leads to **Helm Crag** (see Walk 23), we bear right. 50 yards to the west, another cairn (Wp.20) marks the continuation of the path used in Walk 23, which is currently very muddy but is due to be paved, so should be easy to follow by the time of publication. After crossing a watershed, we climb over a rocky rise then skirt to the left of a small nameless summit, beyond which we cross the path used to descend into **Far Easedale** in Walk 23 (Wp.21 126M).

Maintaining a southwesterly direction on a much fainter way marked by occasional cairns, we climb to the right bank of **Mere Beck**, where there are two large cairns (Wp.22 131M). Still lacking a consistent path, we follow a faint way roughly defined by stubby fencing posts and occasional cairns that

guide us to a shallow gully, at the top of which we again draw alongside the beck (Wp.23 139M).

Climbing across the rocks to the left of the watercourse, we follow the beck to the south on a marginally clearer eroded trail, though there are still a couple of nasty soft patches to be bypassed. Trail and watercourse diverge, and we climb to cross the line of fencing posts (Wp.24 149M). Following the fencing posts, we traverse level ground on **Codale Head** (Wp.25 159M) then drop down into a shallow basin. Skirting to the left of the large marshy area at the heart of the basin, we climb onto the rough pinnacle of **Sergeant Man**, which is capped by a collapsed cairn (Wp.26 167M)

Retracing our steps 100 yards to the east, we descend (SE) on a clear path passing two cairns (Wp.27 173M). After a second pairing of cairns (Wp.28 177M), we head east, soon coming into sight of **Codale Tarn**. A steady descent on a clear path takes us past the junction with the **Codale Tarn** path (Wp.29 187M), after which we follow the same route as Walk 24 for the descent. For a slightly more detailed description, see Walk 24, Wps. 19-25, the key points of which are summarized below.

After a rough cairn-marked descent, the trail crosses stepping stones on marshy ground (Wp.30 199M).

Ignoring a junction to the left at the far end of the lake (Wp.31 206M), we descend alongside **Sourmilk Gill**, passing a small spur doubling back on the left to a large plunge pool (Wp.32 218M). At a signposted crossroads of trails and tracks, we carry straight on (Wp.33 230M) to rejoin the **Easedale Road** (Wp.34 237M), where we turn right, recovering our outward route at Wp.4.

Rejoining the Easedale Road (Wp.34)

Objectively speaking, **Loughrigg Fell** is nothing better than a scruffy bit of upland laced with rather too many paths and lacking a major summit. Subjectively, it's one of the **Lake District's** favourite fells, surrounded by some of the area's most evocative names, splashed with enough shades of brown to give Rembrandt the greeneye, and enjoying views out of all proportion to its modest height and the even more modest effort involved in scaling it.

Scarcely more than a stroll, our version of this popular walk is a salutation itinerary, suitable for making the most of a fine summer's eve on arrival or taking your leave on the morning of departure.

The top's got more paths than a pamphlet on oriental wisdom and, if every way was itemized, it would reduce a map to a plateful of spaghetti, waypointing to an impenetrable splodge of co-ordinates, and description to a left-right-left-right marching chant. For simplicity's sake, we follow the main trail. Unless explicitly stated to the contrary, ignore all junctions. That said, in fine weather you can extend the walk almost indefinitely, roaming at will across the fell's many minor tops and byways.

| 1 | 1.4 H | 2.8 miles/4½km | 250m / 250m | ↻ | 0* |

*Nearest refreshments are in **Skelwith Bridge**, **Grasmere** and **Ambleside**.

Access: by car

We start 600 yards from the A593 on the **Skelwith Bridge** to **Grasmere** road at the junction of the lanes climbing from **Brunt How** and **Skelwith Bridge** itself. There are two lay-bys, each with room for two or three cars, one just north of the junction, the other just south on the **Skelwith Bridge** branch.

Setting off from the main lane just south of the junction, we take the 'Tarn Foot Farm' bridleway (Wp.1 0M), carrying straight on at a junction after 100 yards (Wp.2) for 'Ambleside'.

Ignoring a footpath off to the left 75 yards later (Wp.3), we stay on the main trail, which climbs gently then levels out, following a contour below **Ivy Crag** and passing the first of two shortcuts, just above a TV aerial (Wp.4 9M).

We stick with the main trail until it joins another broad trail (Wp.5 21M) below a tiny tarn, which according to an

Clambering up a mini-cleft of rock.

ephemeral looking sign planted on a crutch by the National Trust, is dubbed a vulgar variant of 'Ordure Lake' (a misguided attempt to update the Trust's image?) and is the source of good luck if you can toss a stone into the tarn from the path. Turning left, we climb northwest, passing a large pile of stones and clambering up a mini-cleft of ragged rock (Wp.6), from the top of which we can see **Ambleside** and enjoy a particularly fine view of the **Fairfield Horseshoe**.

Climbing in a more westerly direction, we pass a second pile of stones (Wp.7 31M), views opening out over **Tilberthwaite**, **Swirl How** and **Wrynose**, then the **Langdale Pikes** and **Crinkle Crags**. 75 yards later (Wp.8), we fork left, detouring onto one of the fell's many mini-peaks, before rejoining the main trail.

The trig point (Wp.9)

Maintaining direction (NW), we pass several more piles of stones before roughly tailored steps take us over a rise that has briefly obscured the views, shortly after which we reach the main peak and the trig point (Wp.9 46M).

Loughrigg Tarn

From the trig point, we double back onto the obvious broad grassy trail just south of the peak, which descends steeply (SW), gradually getting stonier and briefly becoming confused with a watershed. When path and watershed diverge (Wp.10 52M), we fork left, bringing into view **Loughrigg Tarn**.

After a steep, somewhat knee-sandwiching descent, we turn left at a T-junction (Wp.11 59M), bearing left 225 yards later when the path joins a track above the tarn (Wp.12). 100 yards after that, we fork right on a wayposted right-of-way (Wp.13) that traverses a field then crosses the track (Wp.14) into a second field before rejoining our outward route at Wp.3.

Ridges define the **Lake District** walking experience, as a result of which many hikers are so determined to stay on high ground doing classic horseshoes, they ignore the valleys, which is a pity since there's some lovely low lying ground, as you'll see in this simple half-horseshoe, climbing the **Scandale Valley** and returning via **Red Screes** ridge. Given the final stretch on the road, the walk is not recommended at weekends. We start from the mini-roundabout to the north of **Ambleside** at the junction of the **Kirkstone** and **Rydal** roads. The roundabout is next to the town's main car park, which charges £6 for a 9 hour stay.

3	3½ H	7.4 miles/12km	700m / 700m	↻	5

Access: on foot from **Ambleside**

> **Stroll**
> **High Sweden Bridge**
>
> **Short Version**
> **Scandale Bottom**

Approaching High Sweden Bridge

From the roundabout (Wp.1 0M), we take the 'Kirkstone' road, passing **The Golden Rule** pub and 'Chapel House B&B', then turning left on **Sweden Bridge Lane** (Wp.2 3M). Ignoring all branches, including the 'Belle Vue Lane/Low Sweden Bridge' fork on the left and a couple of footpath signs to the right, we follow **Sweden Bridge Lane** till it ends at a wooden gate (Wp.3 9M).

High Sweden Bridge

Going through the gate, we continue on a drovers trail, climbing gently (N) into **Scandale Valley**, at the mouth of which the trail levels off. After traversing lovely mixed woodland above the banks of **Scandale Beck** and passing a couple of cavernous quarries, we emerge at a Y-junction overlooking **High Sweden Bridge** (Wp.4 36M).

For the stroll, bear left here, cross the bridge and climb to Wp.4 of Walk 28, returning to **Ambleside** via **Low Sweden Bridge**. For the main walk, we fork right and continue up the valley on the eastern flank of the beck.

There are no branches and nowhere to go wrong, so I strongly recommend putting the book away and just enjoying the trail, as it winds its way into the

Scandale Bottom

smoothly scooped bay of **Scandale**, drystone walls snaking across the undulating land in such perfect serpentines it's hard to believe they weren't designed according to the governing principles of the picturesque rather than more prosaic, pragmatic considerations.

After crossing a rise, our trail meanders along the fringes of the marshy basin of **Scandale Bottom**, crossing a couple of shallow affluents before reaching a ford in the main beck (Wp.5 64M). We ford another branch of the beck 50 yards later, then follow a slightly fainter trail, keeping the main drystone wall on our right until we pass a sheepfold and go through a wooden gate beside a stone stile (Wp.6 70M).

This would make a convenient stopping point for the Short Version. If the ground's not too wet underfoot, you might also bear left and skirt behind the marsh to follow the intermittent sheep walks down the western flank of the valley.

For the full walk, we maintain a northerly direction, now with the wall on our left, climbing steadily to cross a tumbledown lateral wall, after which, our trail veers right (Wp.7 83M) (NNE). 500 yards later, just short of a ladder stile, we veer right again (SSE), to cross a breach in a wall on **Scandale Pass** (Wp.8 91M).

From here there are a number of options. Following contours, it is

possible to climb to **Middle Dodd** and approach **Red Screes** from the north. Alternatively, one can climb directly to the **Red Screes** trig point. We've opted for a third route, climbing alongside the wall, as it's easier and the simplest to follow when visibility is poor.

Bearing right, we follow the wall, climbing steadily to steeply (S), passing an intersection with a lateral wall rising from **Scandale Valley** (Wp.9 102M). Ignoring a faint fork to the left, we continue climbing on the main trail shadowing the wall. 275 yards later, the gradient eases as we approach the head of our guiding wall, which gradually tapers away then ends at a T-junction with another wall (Wp.10 120M). Ignoring a minor fork to the right, we stay on the main trail as it curves east, slicing across the bland uplands of **Red Screes** before passing a small tarn and reaching the ridge at a tiny rise of rock capped with a cairn (Wp.11 126M), a little way south of the trig point.

Setting off southwest, more or less off-path for the first 100 yards, we pick up a clear, stony trail at a large pile of stones (Wp.12). Maintaining a southwesterly direction in as much as the intermittent muddy patches allow, we cross the remains of a wall (Wp.13 133M) and pass a quarry warning sign above **Snarker Pike** (Wp.14 143M). After meandering through a long marshy area where the path is slightly obscure, we approach a wall on our right, joining a clearer trail (Wp.15 153M) shortly before a ladder stile (Wp.16 155M).

We now follow a broad grassy alley defined by two walls, soon crossing a second ladder stile (Wp.17 164M). From here, we simply stay between the walls all the way to the **Kirkstone Road** (Wp.18 187M). Turning right, we follow the lane down to **Ambleside**, in this instance probably not passing **The Golden Rule**.

28 THE FAIRFIELD HORSESHOE

The most famous if not the most interesting of the **Lake District's** horseshoe itineraries, **Fairfield** is an ideal first outing on higher fells as it's virtually impossible to get lost. I know I'm setting myself up for some irate e-mails there. Everything's possible. I managed to drive into a tree in the Sahara, my sister once sank an 'unsinkable' sailing dinghy, and even the most benign mountains can be disorienting in poor conditions.

Nonetheless, the route really is very straightforward, following a wall virtually all the way up and a 'motorway' path all the way down. The 'motorway' is the result of the walk's popularity and you wouldn't want to be up here during one of the **Lake District's** 'rush hours', but on an ordinary weekday you're unlikely to see more than half a dozen people all day, certainly not enough to spoil the fabulous views, but enough to comfort the novice. We start from the mini-roundabout to the north of **Ambleside** at the junction of the **Kirkstone** and **Rydal** roads. The roundabout is next to the town's main car park, which charges £6 for a 9hour stay.

| 4 | 5H | 11.1 miles/18km | 950m / 950m | ↻ | 5 |

Access: on foot from **Ambleside**

| **Stroll** |
| **Rydal Hall** |

From the roundabout (Wp.1 0M), we take the 'Kirkstone' road, turning left almost immediately on **Nook Lane**. At the end of the lane, we go through the asphalted yard of **Nook End Farm** onto a broad trail fronted by green gates (Wp.2 10M). Ignoring the concrete spur climbing to the right, we cross **Low Sweden Bridge** and embark on a long, gentle climb following a broad, stony trail through three wall-gateways (Wp.3 28M the 3rd gateway). After a fourth gateway, we continue straight ahead at a wayposted junction (Wp.4 36M), climbing steadily on a grassier, but still obvious trail.

The trail becomes rockier below **Brock Crags**, then narrows to a path as we wind onto the ridge and approach the wall on our left. This wall is the one we follow all the way to **Hart Crag**, which means the book can be happily stashed if you don't want to pace progress. When the option arises, you can follow either side of the wall, depending on prevailing winds and conditions underfoot. The main trail favours the eastern side of the wall crossing very muddy patches interrupted by long dry stretches, while the way on the western side of the wall is generally damper but never so muddy.

At a low lateral wall, we pass a waypost indicating a way over the principal wall on our left (Wp.5 52M) - judge which way you go according to conditions. The main trail passes to the right of **Low Pike** then traverses another lateral wall via a ladder stile (Wp.6 72M). It subsequently crosses onto the western side of the guiding wall below **High Pike** (Wp.7 82M), after which we climb across a grassy shoulder, bringing into view the broad sweep of **Fairfield** and **Rydal Head**. After a natural stepover in the guiding wall behind **High Pike** (Wp.8 93M), we climb more gently, and the guiding wall gradually dwindles to a line of rubble as we make our final approach to the pile of stones marking **Dove Crag** (Wp.9 118M).

Approaching Scruffy Crags

Following the remains of the guiding wall (NW), we descend slightly till it peters out in a slew of rocks at the foot of **Hart Crag** (Wp.10 131M). Taking a cairn marked trodden way climbing through the debris to the right of the main rockspill, we pass behind the summit of **Hart Crag** (Wp.11 137M), where fine views open out over **Deepdale** and **St. Sunday Crag**. Following a reasonably clear, cairn marked way curving northwest, we drop down to a more pronounced col beside **Scruffy Crag** (Wp.12 142M), where there's a natural bolt hole tucked under an overhanging boulder.

From the col, we climb on a clear, eroded way over rocks to the western limit of the crags preceding **Fairfield** (Wp.13 150M). This is where the 'motorway' begins, a 10 foot wide stony trail marked by very large cairns. If visibility is poor and you don't have a GPS, as soon as you find yourself walking on grass, you know you're off path. We follow this trail across the grassy expanse of **Fairfield** up to the windbreaks on its flat, stony summit (Wp.14 158M). It's worth detouring to the northern edge of the summit to enjoy the views over **Helvellyn** and **St. Sunday Crag**, which should be enough to have you hurrying off to buy our sister publication, 'Walk! The Lake District (North)' if you haven't already got a copy.

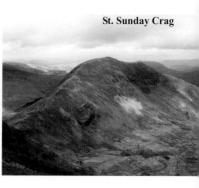
St. Sunday Crag

Descending to Great Rigg

To continue, on what is perhaps the finest part of the walk, we take the 'motorway' south, enjoying fabulous views on all sides, as we descend across **Great Rigg** (Wp.15 176M). A steeper descent takes us past a path forking right (Wp.16 179M), after which we cross a small, unnamed summit, and pass a tiny tarn (Wp.17 199M). Skirting a succession of minor rises, including **Heron Pike**, we descend steadily across the more intricately sculpted southern end of the ridge, passing another branch to the right (Wp.18 220M) 275 yards before crossing a ladder stile (Wp.19).

We then curve southeast off the end of **Nab Scar**, enjoying fine views of **Loughrigg** and **Rydal Cave**, and descend to a northeasterly traverse lined with a flimsy balustrade (Wp.20 237M). A winding descent on a partially paved path leads to another ladder-stile (Wp.21 250M), after which a final steady descent, paved save for the last 100 yards, emerges on a dirt track/concrete lane (Wp.22 260M).

Turning right, we stroll down the lane for a couple of hundred yards then turn left on a signposted track into the 'Rydal Hall Community' (GPS reception is poor here). Following the 'Ambleside' signposted track through the **Rydal Hall** estate, we emerge on the A591 at the gatehouse (Wp.23 285M) and turn left, returning to the start via the road.

Looking back at The Horseshoe

Mini-fell, mini-walk, maxi-fun. Our ascent via **Nanny Lane** says it all really. This is the 'Mary Poppins' of fell walking: pretty, safe, but with a touch of magic about it that will warm the heart of all but the most obdurate. Come to think of it, when I recorded the route there was someone on the ridge with an umbrella! Macho, you won't feel; cheered, you will. Enjoy.

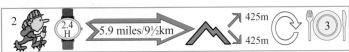

2	2.4 H	5.9 miles/9½km	425m / 425m	3

Access: on foot from **Troutbeck**

Stroll
Nanny Lane, Hundreds Road, Robin Lane (see text)

We start from the small parking area at the foot of the 'Church Bridge/Townend' access lane between **Troutbeck** village and the A592, though the walk can easily be joined from the village itself or **Limefitt** campsite, which is 150 yards up the **Kirkstone** road. A weekend/summer bus service from **Bowness/Windermere** stops at **Troutbeck Church**.

From the parking area (Wp.1 0M), we walk back to the A592 and past the church, behind which we turn left on a signposted bridleway between the churchyard and a playground (Wp.2). At a Y-junction 100 yards later (Wp.3), we fork right to follow a footpath then farm track up to a crossroads with a tarmac lane (Wp.4 12M). Turning left then, after 50 yards, right (Wp.5), we emerge in the village just north of 'Lane Foot Farm' and the signposted turning into 'Nanny Lane' (Wp.6 17M).

Nanny Lane

We take the **Nanny Lane** dirt track, climbing steadily then gently to cross a stile within sight of **Wansfell** (Wp.7 30M). 275 yards later, we reach the junction with the main 'Ambleside via Wansfell' path (Wp.8 35M).

For the stroll, turn left here to pick up the described descent at Wp.15 on the nearside of the next wall.

For the main walk, we continue along **Nanny Lane**, the head of which can be a bit muddy after heavy rain.

At the end of the lane, we cross a ladder-stile to our left (Wp.9 44M), continuing in a northerly direction on a narrow sheepwalk shadowing a wall. Shortly before the corner of the wall, our path crosses a meagre spring and veers left (Wp.10 52M), for a brief but quite steep climb (WNW) to a cairn on the back of the ridge (Wp.11 58M).

Bearing left (SW), we follow a clear, grassy, occasionally marshy path meandering along the ridge, dipping up and down, crossing a distinct little

The stone stile at Wp.13

peak (Wp.12 66M) and a stone stile (Wp.13 73M). The views of **Windermere** from here are particularly fine and we can see to the southeast **Hundreds Road**, the track we use after descending from **Wansfell Pike**, which we reach 500 yards later (Wp.14 83M). The twin nubs of **Wansfell Pike** don't exactly lend the name 'pike' an air of drama, but the view is fabulous.

Doubling back to the left, away from the stile and the path to **Ambleside**, we descend along the main path passed at Wp.8, back toward **Nanny Lane** (E). After going through a kissing gate, we turn right on a wayposted permissive path (Wp.15 95M) traversing open moor to a stone stile beside a gate (Wp.16 101M) then onto the **Hundreds Road** dirt track (Wp.17 104M).

Onto the Hundreds Road (Wp.17)

Bearing left, we follow **Hundreds Road**, which becomes **Robin Lane**, also a dirt track, at an inverted Y-junction (Wp.18 118M). We stay on the main track, south-east then east, carrying straight on (the left fork) at a Y-junction cradling a bench (Wp.19 124M). Arriving in **Troutbeck** beside the Post Office, we bear left and take the lane descending past **Granary Cottage** (Wp.20 135M) back to our starting point.

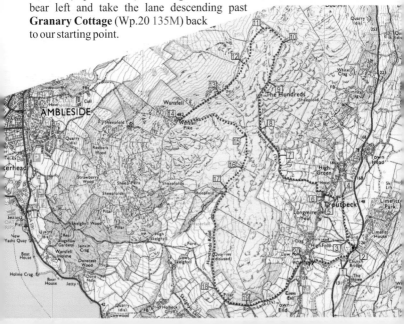

A lovely valley/ridge combination, in this instance blessed by a particularly spectacular stretch of ridge and a descent on the lower, less frequently walked section of **High Street**, the old Roman 'road' linking forts at **Ambleside** and **Penrith**. The way down to **Hagg Gill** is also known as **Scot's Rake**, in honour of medieval raiders from north of the border, whose rustling activities were greatly facilitated by the strategically placed Roman road. Always supposing you don't have a party of wild and woolly Picts bearing down on you intent on a little light plundering, **Hagg Gill** is a delightfully peaceful place and an excellent spot for a picnic at the end of the stroll. For the stroll, do the main walk till Wp.4 then turn left and follow the described track/trail in reverse to Wp.18. The ridge is exposed and not recommended in high winds or when visibility is poor.

Access: on foot from **Troubeck**

> **Stroll**
> **Hagg Gill**

We start from the small parking area at the foot of the 'Church Bridge/Townend' access lane between **Troubeck** village and the A592, though the walk can easily be joined from the village itself (descending via the lane in front of the post office or across the fields from **Nanny Lane** see Walk 29) or from **Limefitt** campsite (take the bridleway to the right of the campsite pub up to Wp.24 then turn right to reach Wp.4). A weekend/summer bus service from **Bowness/Windermere** stops at **Troubeck Church**.

Troubeck Valley from the south

From the parking area (Wp.1 0M), we walk back to the A592 and follow it south for a little under 75 yards, then turn left on a signposted bridleway (Wp.2), which follows a broad, badly eroded track known as the **Garburn Road**. After a steep climb, the track veers right briefly, passing a couple of farms before resuming a more easterly direction.

We follow this track all the way to **Garburn Pass**, staying on the main track at every junction, ignoring two branches accessing the **Longmire Road** track on our right (Wp.3 13M), a fork on the left 100 yards later (Wp.4), the **Dubbs Road** track doubling back to the right (Wp.5 25M), and a minor branch into a wood on our right (Wp.6 30M). Eventually, the **Garburn Road** levels out and goes through a gate onto the western end of **Garburn Pass** at the foot of the ridge, which has been visible throughout most of the ascent. 100 yards after the gate, we turn left on a broad trail marked by a large pile of stones (Wp.7 54M).

Climbing northeast toward the **Yoke**, the first summit on the ridge, we follow a clear cairn-marked trail passing to the left of a small crag, where there's a sturdy post loosely planted in the turf (Wp.8 69M). Passing a second post behind the crag, we maintain direction (NE), approaching a wall within sight of **Harter Fell** and **Kentmere Pike**, and climb alongside the wall (N) to a ladder-stile (Wp.9 81M).

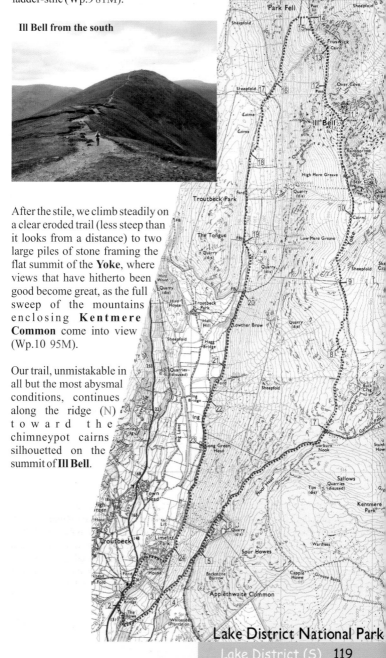

Ill Bell from the south

After the stile, we climb steadily on a clear eroded trail (less steep than it looks from a distance) to two large piles of stone framing the flat summit of the **Yoke**, where views that have hitherto been good become great, as the full sweep of the mountains enclosing **Kentmere Common** come into view (Wp.10 95M).

Our trail, unmistakable in all but the most abysmal conditions, continues along the ridge (N) toward the chimneypot cairns silhouetted on the summit of **Ill Bell**.

Lake District National Park

Kentmere Reservoir

After a negligible descent (around 100 ft), an easy but steep climb (our steepest yet) brings us onto the summit of **Ill Bell** (Wp.11 111M).

From the northern end of the summit, we take a steep, stony path descending rapidly toward the dramatic sweep of **Over Cove**.

Ignoring a minor, slightly vertiginous looking path that forks left across the head of **Blue Gill** (Wp.12 121M), we stay on the main trail, traversing the exposed summit of **Froswick** (Wp.13 129M) and descending toward the col above **Wander Scar**.

When the WNW descent off **Froswick** bottoms out beyond the northern fold shielding **Blue Gill**, we turn left (Wp.14 135M) leaving the clear trail and cutting across a grassy slope (W), essentially off path for 100 yards, to join **Scot's Rake** (Wp.15), discernible during the descent as a narrow white path. Turning left again, we descend steadily (SW then S) across **Park Fell** toward the swell of **Troutbeck Tongue** and the immaculately sculpted landscape stretching away to **Windermere**.

The trail eventually curves right (SSW), descending to merge with another path shadowing a wall (Wp.16 154M). We continue descending on a broad grassy trail defined by the wall and **Blue Gill**, down to a weighted gate alongside the gill (Wp.17 158M), where the broad trail apparently peters out amid patchy marsh grass. Maintaining direction (SW), we find a faint way that soon becomes clearer, bearing south and feeding into an indistinct farm track, which we follow to a ford over **Hagg Gill**, where we join a clear track (visible throughout the descent) along the eastern flank of **Troutbeck Tongue** (Wp.18 166M). We follow this track to the south, passing a branch doubling back on the right 100 yards later.

After a little over half a mile on the track, we bear left at a Y-junction (Wp.19 179M) and descend to cross a footbridge below a farm building. Following a grassy track along the left bank of **Hagg Gill**, we pass below a couple of large heaps of spoil, and go through the higher of two gates above a second footbridge (Wp.20 188M). The track dwindles to a path for several hundred yards, then broadens again, becoming a clear farm track at a metal gate (Wp.21 198M).

After going through another gate, we join a partially metalled track (Wp.22 204M). Maintaining a southerly direction, we follow this track to **Long Green Head Farm**. Passing to the left of the farm, we go through a gate (Wp.23 208M) onto a slightly more attractive track, climbing some 60 feet, after which the track levels off and becomes a broad trail running alongside the fence behind **Limefitt** campsite. At a Y-junction (Wp.24 223M), we bear right and follow the bridleway signs down through the campsite, back to the road, 150 yards from our starting point.

31 A KENDAL ROUND

A walk on the tame side exploring the pastoral countryside surrounding **Kendal**. Ideal as a first outing for getting your bearings or as an alternative to the high fells during bad weather. The relatively high exertion rating is for distance rather than any concerted effort involved in the actual walking. For Stroll (b), access is clearer from the more westerly of the two car parks on the **Underbarrow Road**. The route from the river up to **Helsington Church** is a little obscure, but after **Helsington Barrows**, there are at least half a dozen obvious paths traversing **Scout Scar**, all equally viable, and the book can be put away if you prefer to enjoy the views rather than read directions.

3 | 4H | 9.8 miles/16km | 250m / 250m | 5

Strolls
(a) Hawes Bridge follow the main footpath past Wp.6 to **Hawes Bridge** then return to **Kendal** along the left bank of the river.
(b) Cunswick Scar from Wp.19
(c) Scout Scar from Wp.19 (in reverse)

Access: on foot from **Kendal**

We start from the Tourist Information Office in the centre of **Kendal**, chosen for ease of location rather than any particular aesthetic merit. If you happen to be arriving by car, there are numerous car parks in the centre of town, but it's worth noting that parking in the residential roads south of **Romney Bridge** (Wp.2) is unrestricted, free, and plentiful, even on a Bank Holiday weekend.

Taking the narrow road descending to the right of the **Tourist Information Centre** (Wp.1 0M), we stroll down to the river and turn right on 'Riverside Walk'. Following the riverbank, we pass a footbridge to **Kendal Castle** and a road bridge. Staying on the right bank of the river, we bear left into 'South Street' and left again at the 'West Street' housing complex.

After 'Romney Bridge' (Wp.2 21M), the river traces a chicane round the waterworks, within sight of **Scout Scar**. At a Y-junction (Wp.3 36M), we fork left into **Scroggs Wood**, skirting the last area of housing. We then cross a lane (Wp.4 44M) into open country and take a right of way cutting across a field, signposted 'Hawes Bridge'.

Scroggs Wood

On the far side of the first pasture, we take the narrower of two gated exits, and traverse a second pasture to rejoin the riverbank at a broken wooden stile in a dry stone wall (Wp.5 52M). Continuing along the riverbank, we go through a kissing gate and three stone stiles. Immediately after the third stone stile (Wp.6 66M), we turn right, following the fence/hedge away from the river toward the **Prizet Farm** hamlet (W).

At the far end of a large green farm building, we cross the tip of a lane (Wp.7 68M). Clambering over two wooden stiles, we traverse a small field to the left of a long bungalow, then re-cross the lane to follow a right of way through more pasture down to a lodge house on the A6, just north of the BP garage. On the far side of the road (which is fast but easily crossed), we follow a right-of-way for 'Briggs House Farm' (Wp.8 75M).

Climbing gently, we cross a succession of stiles to reach a broad flat pasture (Wp.9 82M). Traversing this and a second flat pasture, we access the **Brigg House Farm** lane via a metal gate (Wp.10 90M). Crossing the lane, we climb a second metal gate (the hasp is too tight too open) and bear right toward **Briggs House Farm**. At the top of the field, a right-of-way arrow indicates our way behind **Briggs House Farm** onto a tarmac lane, where we turn left, passing **Waingale** bungalow.

The lane rapidly dwindles to an unmetalled track, which takes us back into fields, going through two metal gates. We leave the track when it swings left through a third gate and continue along the right hand side of the stone wall to a coppice concealing a fourth gate (Wp.11 106M). Squeezing through the narrow gap to the left of the gate, we maintain a westerly direction alongside the wall, crossing a small rise before descending to a lane beside **Helsington Church**, where there's a location board (Wp.12 112M) and several benches with fine views of the **Lyth Valley** and **Whitbarrow Scar**.

Turning right, we stroll along the lane to the **Brigsteer Road** where, 25 yards to our right, a 'Scout Scar' signpost indicates the way across the National Trust property of 'Helsington Barrows' (Wp.13 118M). Following a broad grassy trail, we climb gently across heathland, leaving the National Trust land via a kissing gate (Wp.14 126M). The trail levels out before curling round to the right and dipping into a wooded dell. Carrying straight on at a crossroads of paths (Wp.15 131M), we climb to a second crossroads on the edge of the scar. We can take either of the two paths to the left. The lower path hugs the verge of the scar, while the higher path (followed by our trackline) climbs alongside a dry stone wall (NE) toward the broad back of the fell. Nearing the brow of the hill, we veer left at a triple fork (Wp.16 140M), traversing undulating upland (N) to a confluence of trails around a trig point (Wp.17 151M), within sight of the domed **Scout Scar** shelter.

Going through a gap in the wall behind the trig point, we follow the main trail to the north, bearing left as we pass another kissing gate to climb to the shelter (Wp.18 162M), the roof of which serves as a locator board for the **Lake District** fells, as well as the **Howgills**, the **Yorkshire Dales**, and the **Forest of Bowland**. Taking any of the well-trodden trails to the north, we descend to the **Underbarrow Road** and the main car park (Wp.19 169M) below the telecommunications mast.

At the entrance to the car park, a narrow path on the right curves round the eastern side of the antenna to a kissing gate, beyond which we follow a signposted footpath bearing ENE across rolling pasture. After crossing **Gamblesmire Lane** (Wp.20 181M), we resume a more northerly direction, descending toward a shallow depression just below the final rise of **Cunswick Fell**. Shortly before the descent bottoms out, we come to a fence breached by two stiles. We use the stile on the right and follow the wall on the right as it curves behind the final rise till we reach a narrow stone stile backed by a waypost (Wp.21 198M).

Going through the stile and traversing the next field, we come to the A591, which we cross via a footbridge with a ladder-stile at either end (Wp.22 207M). After climbing alongside its perimeter, we enter **Kendal Fell** golf course (Wp.23 214M), and follow a well trodden, wayposted path, crossing the golf course and bringing **Kendal** into view. Immediately after leaving the golf course, the path divides and we fork left (Wp.24 224M), descending onto a trail alongside the last fields above the town. Maintaining direction (SE), we follow this trail to the end of a lane (Wp.25 228M).

At the bottom of the lane, we turn right on **Queen's Road** then left 100 yards later at the junction with **Serpentine Road**, where we take a partially stepped pedestrian alley. When this alley rejoins the road, we descend to the right for 30 feet to another pedestrian alley.

This alley, **Fountain Brow**, crosses another narrow road and the lower entrance to **Booths' Shopping Centre** before emerging on the high street, 50 yards north of the clock tower above the Tourist Information Centre.

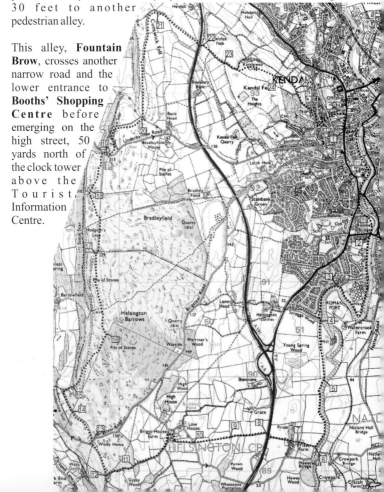

32 WHITBARROW

Whitbarrow, the long, low fell on the western flank of the **Lyth Valley**, is normally approached from it's dramatic western edge, but given the glut of drama to be had elsewhere in the **Lake District**, we've opted for a gentler ascent via the delightfully varied woodland on its eastern side. There's scant logic to the full route, which meanders about like a python in a pinball machine, but the contrasting scenery justifies our winding course and is sufficiently varied to make it worth incorporating the short version (see text) within the full walk.

2 | (3H) | 6.6 miles/11 km | 200m / 200m | ↻ | 2*

*The **Lyth Valley Hotel** is 375 yards north of the **Row** turn-off. If you're staying at the hotel, **Row** can be reached via the bridleway beginning in front of the hotel

Short Version
W h i t b a r r o w
Woods (see text)

Access: by car

The walk starts in the hamlet of **Row**, signposted from the A5074 between the coast and **Bowness on Windermere**. If you're driving from **Kendal**, take the **Underbarrow** road then turn left on the slip road within sight of **Crosthwaite** church, joining the A5074 750 yards north of the **Row** turn-off. There's limited but adequate parking alongside the road in the centre of the hamlet.

Township Plantation

From the centre of **Row** (Wp.1 0M), we take the lane forking left between **Row Farm** and **Row Barn**, immediately passing **Byremount View**. At the end of the lane, we go through a wooden gate between a white cottage and an apple orchard. Following the wall on our left, we skirt a large pasture, climbing gently to a wooden gate into **Township Plantation** wood, where we pass a waypost (Wp.2 13M). Ignoring the path climbing to the right, we continue along the lower edge of the wood, passing several branch paths before joining a dirt track at a Y-junction (Wp.3 22M). Taking the left hand fork of the Y-junction, we maintain our southerly direction.

The track dwindles to a path going through a wooden gate in a wall, 50 yards after which we join a waymarked path climbing from the left (Wp.4 30M). Continuing to the south, we fork left 20 yards later, following a broader trail through more mature, managed woodland to a junction with a clear dirt track (Wp.5 34M) below several towering oaks.

If you wish to climb directly onto the uplands, turn right here, rejoining the described itinerary at Wp.11. Otherwise, we continue south to a staggered junction (Wp.6 36M).

Turning right then immediately left, we follow the wayp0sted route (S) until we come to a crossroads of dirt tracks just after an immense conifer (Wp.7 65M). We leave the waypostred route here, turning right and climbing across a small rise before dipping down to a muddy Y-junction (Wp.8 71M). Forking right, we climb through fairytale forest that's partly paved with mossy boulders, several of them clasped between the toes of exposed clawlike roots. After a steady climb, our trail levels out and curves NNW, descending slightly to pass a small sinkhole (Wp.9 86M). A second long descent through more open woodland leads to a Y-junction (Wp.10 100M) a couple of hundred yards from our outward route. Branching left, we join the trail climbing from Wp.5.

For a short walk, turn right to rejoin our outward route at Wp.5. For the full walk, we turn left and climb to a major path forking right (Wp.11 104M), which leads to the great bare fell of 'Whitbarrow National Nature Reserve' (Wp.12 108M). Bearing left, we traverse **Flodder Allotment** on a broad grassy trail climbing to **Lord's Seat** (Wp.13 120M), unmistakable with its squat, rounded memorial pillar.

Two major trails marked with large piles of stones branch out from here, one to the South, one to the West. We follow the route to the West for 325 yards until it bears left (SW) and descends off the scar (Wp.14 126M), at which point we fork right to follow a series of faint cow paths through the windswept birch woods to the North. These paths frequently peter out, but so long as you maintain a northerly direction and don't lose any significant altitude, there's little risk of getting lost.

After crossing two distinct patches of woodland, the path becomes clearer and descends to the entrance of a mine just above **Bell Rake** (Wp.15 142M), where we turn right (E) to follow a high dry stone wall defining the northern limit of the nature reserve (NB so long as you remain on the uplands, you'll reach this wall sooner or later, so don't worry about following the 'right' path on what is a rather featureless fell). Following the stone wall, we reach a ladder-stile in the northeastern corner of the reserve (Wp.16 151M).

Once over the stile, we take the main grassy track, which initially heads northwest before gradually curving east to a gateway into a small plantation of pine (Wp.17 160M). Sticking with the waypostred track, we descend to rejoin our outward route at Wp.3 (165M), where we turn left, following the main path back through **Township Plantation**, taking particular care to ignore the forks descending to the right.

A walk for all seasons into the upper reaches of the **River Kent** valley, in which the sort of effort ordinarily associated with a Sunday afternoon stroll in the park is rewarded with a real sense of high mountain wilderness. Highly recommended. We start from the small honesty box 'Institute' parking area just past **Kentmere Church**, which is reached from the A591 via **Staveley**. Parking is very limited in **Kentmere**, so if you're walking at weekends it's best to arrive early.

* Nearest refreshments are in **Staveley**.

Access: car or (summer service) bus from **Staveley**

Kentmere Valley from the Tongue

From the 'Institute' car park (Wp.1 0M), we take the 'Kentmere Reservoir' track behind the church, going through a wayposted gate at the entrance to **Capplerigg** house to join a track up the valley. The track passes 'Brow Head' farm and goes through a gate beside a house with a studded wooden door (Wp.2 7M).

Low Lane

A little over 150 yards later (Wp.3), we go through a narrow gap in the wall on our right and cross a waymarked footbridge (Wp.4), immediately after which we bear left and climb to a stone stile accessing the **Low Lane** trail, where we again turn left (Wp.5 12M).

When the trail crosses an affluent of the **River Kent** and broadens to a track (Wp.6 19M), we fork left, leaving the main track and continuing on a grassy bridleway following a line of telegraph poles, the first of which is waymarked.

When this trail in turn broadens to a dirt track climbing toward **Hallow Bank**, we bear left (Wp.7 23M) maintaining a northerly direction on a path that joins a dirt track beside **Overend Farm** 325 yards later. At a signposted Y-junction behind **Overend**, we fork left for 'Kentmere Reservoir' (Wp.8 30M), following a farm track that goes through a succession of gates and passes a pretty little stone bridge spanning the river (Wp.9 40M).

When the track ends at the gate of a rather grand farm building, **Tongue House** (Wp.10 53M), we cross the farmyard in order to maintain a northerly direction on a much rougher track beginning behind the building. After crossing a ladderstile (Wp.11 62M), we climb amid immense heaps of quarry spoil, following a clear but narrow path running alongside the rocky course of the river to an overflow channel at the eastern end of the dam wall (Wp.12 88M).

If the weather's fine, the reservoir is a great place to linger over a picnic or extend the walk with a stroll round its shoreline. Otherwise, we can either cross the dam wall or follow the very narrow but obvious path cutting across the slope below the dam, then descend (SE) alongside the fence above the weir to a wooden footbridge (Wp.13 93M).

Crossing the bridge, we take a dirt track descending past **Reservoir Cottage** to a concrete bridge over an affluent (Wp.14 111M).

After crossing an exposed rise and skirting behind a wood above **Hartrigg** farm, our track becomes a metalled lane (Wp.15 126M). We stay on this lane for just over half a mile, till it passes a cattle grid, immediately after which we bear left on a signposted footpath for 'Kentmere Church' (Wp.16 143M).

Following a delightful but all too brief grassy trail, we traverse a small rise striated with tumbledown walls and spotted with large boulders, soon joining the track climbed after Wp.2. We can either follow this track back to the start or cross a waymarked stile (Wp.17 153M) down to a lower track, which rejoins the road just east of the church.

The rather undistinguished rises of **Kentmere Pike** and **Harter Fell** are normally included in long horseshoe routes starting from **Sadgill** or **Kentmere**, but in our itinerary the ridge is merely a pretext for the descent! The really dramatic bits of the classic **Kentmere Horseshoe** are covered in Walks 30&37. In our present walk, we climb to **Harter Fell** on an otherwise bland ridge blessed with grand views, then descend from **Nan Bield Pass** along a lovely, beautifully graded path that is such a constant pleasure you begin to wish it would never end. On a fine day, simply exquisite.

We start from the small honesty-box 'Institute' car park just past **Kentmere Church**, which is reached from the A591 via **Staveley**. Parking is very limited in Kentmere, so best to arrive early.

Access: by car or (Summer service) bus from **Staveley**
Stroll: see Wp.7. * Nearest refreshments are in Staveley

From the parking area (Wp.1 0M), we walk back down the 'main' road, turning left on the 'Maggs Howe' B&B lane (Wp.2 4M). 150 yards later, we turn right for 'Green Quarter' on the second of two signposted footpaths (Wp.3). Climbing steadily, we traverse a stand of trees and a small pasture before emerging at a junction of lanes, where we take the lane signed 'Maggs Howe/Longsleddale' (Wp.4). The lane ends at 'The Old Forge' where we go through a gate on our right (Wp.5 13M) onto a waymarked footpath.

Enjoying fine views up the valley, we follow a rough farm track, climbing steadily then gently until the track levels off altogether and becomes fainter as it winds across undulating pasture to a ladder-stile (Wp.6 32M). Maintaining a northeasterly direction on an intermittent path, we come to a couple of gates, where we cross the main **Kentmere/Sadgill** track (Wp.7 42M).

For a stroll, turn left here and take the main track back to **Kentmere**. For the full walk, we climb toward the wall bisecting the ridge (NNW), following a narrow path but detouring as required round a couple of damp patches. The path traces several short doglegs to break the gradient of the first steady climb to reach the ridge behind **Wray Crag** (Wp.8 56M). Continuing along a clear, occasionally boggy trail, we wind through several minor knots of rock, staying around 100 yards from the wall, until path and wall converge for a steeper climb passing **Shipman Knotts**, bringing into view the smooth rise of **Kentmere Pike** (Wp.9 76M).

After crossing a ladder stile (Wp.10 82M), we follow a broad grassy trail climbing (NW) to shadow a fence that, apart from a stretch on **Kentmere Pike**, now replaces the wall. A long gentle climb brings us onto a plateau (Wp.11 98M), where we continue alongside the last bit of wall, passing a large pile of stones amid tiny outcrops of rock marking the high point of **Kentmere**

Pike (Wp.12 101M). After descending to the minor depression of **Brown Howe**, a long gentle haul (following the fence all the way) takes us past the solitary rusting tripod of an old fencing post on **The Knowe** (Wp.13 121M), from where we see **Nan Bield Pass** for the first time.

Ignoring a faint path cutting across the fell toward the pass, we continue along the fence (N) to a large pile of stones, the principle distinguishing feature of **Harter Fell** apart from the fine views to the north (Wp.14 129M). Turning left, we follow cairns across the fell (W) to a superb 'eyrie' overlooking the pass, **Kentmere Reservoir**, **Small Water**, **Haweswater** and the grand sweep of **High Street** (Wp.15). A steady, slightly exposed descent across rough terrain fractured by large boulders and fin like rocks takes us down to the windbreak on **Nan Bield Pass**, where we turn left (Wp.16 146M).

Following a clear path, we snake our way down to the smooth flank of **Kentmere Common** where we cross a myriad of springs and watersheds feeding the reservoir. After traversing a patch of close-cropped grass behind a mini-crag overlooking the dam wall, the first of the **Smallthwaite Knotts** (Wp.17 172M), we cross a rise, bringing the lower reaches of **Kentmere Valley** into view. A gentle descent across the back of the **Tongue** dividing the main valley from **Ullstone Gill** takes us across a marshy area where the path is faint but still discernible. Recovering a clear path (Wp.18 182M), we descend more steeply to the left of **Tongue Scar**, eventually crossing a narrow footbridge over **Ullstone Gill** (Wp.19 193M).

Kentmere Reservoir & Ill Bell

We now follow a drovers' trail running parallel to the track used in the outward leg of Walk

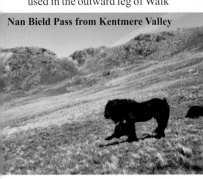
Nan Bield Pass from Kentmere Valley

33, which we eventually join just short of **Overend Farm**. Going through a waymarked metal gate on the left of the farm, we join a bridleway (Wp.20 215M). We turn right at a T-junction with a dirt track a little under 350 yards later (Wp.21) then take the signposted bridleway for 'Kentmere' 300 yards after that (Wp.22 226M). The bridleway, which is initially a track, goes through a gate and dwindles to a trail. 45 yards after a second gate, we turn right, crossing a stone stile (Wp.23 233M) and descend to a footbridge, on the far side of which, we turn left on a dirt track (Wp.24), then fork right at a Y-junction 200 yards later (Wp.25) to return to our starting point.

Despite being dammed, fenced off, hemmed in by prohibition, and having a submerged village lurking about somewhere under its surface, **Haweswater** is one of the more remote and wilder of the region's large lakes. No boats, no cottages, no caravan parks, no campsites, no ice-cream vans, no 'entertainments', rarely any crowds, just one road, one hotel, and a whole lot of good walking.

The tour of the reservoir is ideal as a longish walk in wild weather when higher ground is under cloud, or on a fine day for those who like to stretch their legs without straining their lungs. GPS reception is poor at the start, but improves once we're clear of the trees.

Short Version
The west shore (see introductory notes)

*see note in Area Introduction

Access: by car and bus.
To reach the start by car, follow the signs for 'Haweswater' from **Shap** on the A6, then turn right for 'Burnbanks' after **Bampton**. There's room for several carefully parked cars in the lay-by at the entrance to the hamlet. Buses from **Penrith** run on Tuesdays and Saturdays, with an extended service on Sundays and public holidays between 24th July and 29th August continuing to **Mardale Head**, giving the option of a shorter linear walk avoiding the stretch on the road.

From the entrance to **Burnbanks**, we take the footpath for 'Naddle Bridge' (0M), which traverses a lovely but all too brief oak forest carpeted with bluebells and moss. Turning right when we join the **Mardale Head** road (5M), we follow the road for three quarters of a mile until we see a signpost on our right for 'Lakeshore footpath/Mardale Head' (Wp.1 32M).

And that, strictly speaking, apart from the understanding that the walk is both feasible and desirable, is all you really need to know, since we now simply follow clear footpaths circling the reservoir, which is nearly always within sight and visible even in the worst weather. What follows is therefore purely for the purposes of timekeeping.

The path winds through an enchanting forest of birch bedded in bracken and moss, then narrows as the road curves in to hug the shoreline, obliging us to cross a succession of railway sleeper mini-bridges over drainage outlets.

After crossing a fully fledged footbridge over a minor torrent (Wp.2 63M), we meander along a grassy bank below the **Haweswater Hotel**. A second bridge (Wp.3 72M) leads to more open land within sight of **Mardale Head**. We then cross a third bridge and the grassy access to a slipway before joining a well stabilized track (Wp.4 78M), at the end of which we recover our narrow path, now some way below the road.

After traversing broad, bracken covered slopes below low crags, we pass a signposted junction with the **Old Corpse Road** climbing to 'Swindale' (see Walk 36) (Wp.5 97M). Crossing a narrow stone bridge over the awkwardly named **Rowantreethwaite Beck**, we go through a succession of gateways in decaying walls rising from the submerged village of **Mardale Green**.

Rowntreethwaite Beck

Road and path gradually converge for the final approach to the **Mardale Head** car park, 50 yards behind which, we turn right at a triple fork (Wp.6 118M) and descend to a broad footbridge over **Mardale Beck** (Wp.7 121M), where we turn right again.

Ignoring a minor path forking left 400 yards later (Wp.8), we cross a small rise behind a plantation of pine, then descend (NW) to footbridges over **Riggindale** (Wp.9 143M) and **Randale Becks**.

After descending almost to the water's edge, a brief but steady climb (not as steep as it looks) takes us past **Flakehowe Crags** (Wp.10 157M) from where a gentle descent leads to our next footbridge over **Whelter Beck** (Wp.11 165M).

Subsequent to a brief ascent, our path, now somewhat imperfectly fenced, traverses the **Whelter Knotts** rockslide. After a long, largely level stretch interrupted by the occasional, very minor climb, the shore is masked by mixed woodland, and we ford the shallow watersheds between **Laythwaite** and **Nook Sikes** (Wp.12 181M).

700 yards later, views open out again across the reservoir and we descend to cross a stone-slab footbridge beside a small walled wood on **Pultsgill Sike**, some 450 yards short of our last bridge, a broad concrete structure crossing **Measand Beck** (Wp.13 198M).

After the beck, our path becomes a narrow dirt track, which we follow all the way back to **Burnbanks**, ignoring a fork on the left toward the end (Wp.14 224M) and descending through a couple of gates onto the end of the road through the hamlet.

Seen with the naked eye from below and the mind's eye on the map, the fells of **Selside** and **Branstree** look like a large waste of space, bland grassy uplands and widespaced contour lines holding little promise of interesting walking. But as most walkers will know, 'interesting' walking often means you're so busy looking at the 'interesting' places you're putting your feet, you end the day with only the haziest notion of where you might have been and what you might have been meant to see. By contrast, these two small summits are a sort of end of the pier attraction: it's not the butler we're interested in, but what the butler saw.

And what a sight it is: **Swindale**, the **Pennines**, the desolate **Shap Fells**, the **Howgills**, **Haweswater**, **Longsleddale**, **High Street** and its satellite summits... the list goes on. And in this instance, the objectively 'uninteresting' walking translates as an opportunity to forget about your feet and just enjoy the views.

There's a brief off-path section and a stretch that might as well be, which along with the lack of more immediate interest mean the walk is not recommended during poor visibility, but otherwise it's an easy itinerary, only earning it's high exertion rating for the steep climb away from the lake on the **Old Corpse Road**. The start is reached as per Walk 35 except that we pass the **Burnbanks** turning and stay on the **Haweswater** road till it ends at **Mardale Head.**

4 | 2½ H | 6 miles/9.6 km | 520m / 520m | 0*

* see note in Area Introduction

Access: by car and (Sundays and public holidays 24th July to 29th August) bus from **Penrith**

The lakeside path

From the entrance to the car park at the end of the **Haweswater** road, we squeeze through a narrow gap in the wall (Wp.1 0M) and follow the lakeshore path alongside the road (NE), going through the first of several wall gateways (Wp.2 10M), a reminder of the time when this was pasture for the livestock of **Mardale Green**, the village now submerged in the reservoir.

Another trace of the village is located by our next waypoint, when we cross a stone footbridge over **Rowantreethwaite Beck**, beyond which a sign for 'Swindale' (Wp.3 24M) marks the **Old Corpse Road** from the days when **Mardale** buried its dead in **Shap**.

Turning right, we climb steeply (you wouldn't want to be carrying a coffin up here), crossing the road 80 yards later (Wp.4). The steep climb continues alongside the beck, veering left (NNE) three times to break the gradient, passing a cone-like cairn on a rock on the second northeasterly traverse (Wp.5 36M) and a couple of roofless ruins on the third (Wp.6 41M).

The second ruin

The gradient eases after the ruins as we approach the first of several wayposts (Wp.7 47M), beyond which it levels off altogether. Following the wayposts and the occasional ancient waystone, which doubtless came in handy when the bereaved were weaving their way back from a wake on a dark winter's day, we traverse open moorland, bringing **Shap's** remaining industrial plant into view at the fourth waypost. We then descend very slightly to the fifth waypost (Wp.8 60M), where we turn sharp right on a faint grassy trail climbing south.

The trail curves southwest, then resumes its southerly trajectory, climbing gently onto **Selside End** and passing to the right of a tiny jumble of stones that might once have been arranged in a semblance of a windbreak (Wp.9 66M), albeit a very long time ago. We then pass to the right of the small **Blake Dodd** rise, where views over the full sweep of the **Shap Fells** open out.

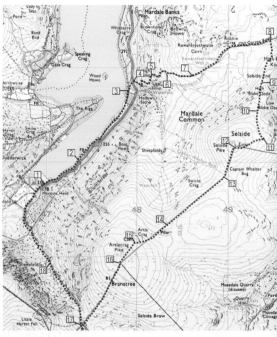

25 yards later, we fork left (SSE) at a faint Y-junction (Wp.10 70M), the better to appreciate the fine view over **Swindale** to the northeast. Reaching a small corrugated iron box framed by four fencing posts (Wp.11 74M), we turn right (off-path) and climb (W) towards a fence, at the corner of which a large windbreak marks the otherwise undistinguished summit of **Selside Pike** (Wp.12 80M), though how it got to be called a 'pike' is anybody's guess; anything less pike-like is hard to imagine.

With one brief and obvious detour, this fence is our guiding line all the way to **Gatescarth Pass**, so if you haven't fallen desperately in love with my prose, put the book away sharpish and just enjoy the views.

Descending off Gatescarth Pass

Following the fence (S), we descend to a muddy scar (Wp.13 84M), after which views over **Haweswater** open out to our right. Continuing along the fence, we head for the distinctive beehive cairns silhouetted against the skyline on **Branstree**.

Dipping down into a second small depression, we see a pillar off to our left, a remnant of the engineering infrastructure from the days when the **Haweswater** dam was being built (Wp.14 95M). We continue alongside the fence a little longer, then gradually bear west along a natural way leading to the beehive cairns (Wp.15 103M).

A reasonably clear path trending back toward the fence (SW) takes us past the circular base of a survey post on **Artlecrag Pike** (another abuse of language) (Wp.16 108M), after which we simply descend alongside the fence to **Gatescarth Pass**, immediately before which we have to pick our way across a patch of bog using the marsh grass as stepping 'stones' - not entirely adequate, I admit, but needs must. At the junction of major trails on the pass (Wp.17 119M), we turn right for a straightforward descent (N) on a broad, stony, unmistakable bridleway, passing a sheepfold (Wp.18 131M) before meandering down alongside **Gatescarth Beck** back to our starting point.

A fitting end to the book, for though **High Street** is no great culminating point in a physical sense, it is widely considered one of the finest walks in the **Lake District**. Climbing via **Small Water**, another Lakeland location that pulls off a surprisingly plausible Pyrenean impersonation, we visit the mini-summit of **Mardale Ill Bell**, then skirt the watersheds feeding the **River Kent**. Finally, after strolling along the Neolithic ridge route that became the Roman road or 'street' linking forts at **Penrith** and **Ambleside**, we descend via the spectacular **Riggindale** spur, until recently home to England's only pair of nesting Golden Eagles.

Spare a thought though for the poor legionnaires who once walked **High Street**. You and I may think it's a wonderful place, but you can't help wondering how the common foot soldier felt about a posting to this remote spot on the periphery of the civilized world. Italy, North Africa, Gaul, the Iberian peninsula... all were billets in bountiful lands beckoning the sun-loving centurion. But empire being what it is, somebody had to come north and guard windswept fells with nothing but a bit of a cloak, a pair of sandals, a bottle of garum and a conviction of imperial superiority to keep the cold out. I hate to think what they made of 'Britannia Inferior', the northern province of which **Cumbria** was a part.

| 4 | 3H | 6 miles/9.6 km | 625m / 625m | ↻ | 0* |

**Stroll
Small Water**

* see note in Area Introduction

Access: by car and (Sundays & Public Holidays 24/7 to 29/8) bus from **Penrith**

Starting from the end of the **Haweswater** road (see Walks 35&36 for access), we go through the kissing gate directly behind the car park (Wp.1 0M) and take the central path at the triple-fork 45yards from the gate (Wp.2).

A gentle climb on a broad trail brings us to a second kissing gate (Wp.3 5M) and a finely sculpted landscape, mottled with outcrops of layered rock that looks like it's only recently been pressed together and that by a somewhat inexpert hand. After going through a third, conventional gate (Wp.4 16M), we climb steadily alongside **Small Water Beck**, which we cross via a stone footbridge (Wp.5 24M) for the final climb to **Small Water** (Wp.6 31M), a great spot for a picnic at the end of a stroll.

Small Water

For the full walk, we bear right and continue round the north-western side of the lake, passing (a rarity in the Lake District) three, roofed stone shelters (see picture on next page) and a tumbledown cairn where the climbing resumes

Small Water shelter

(Wp.7 36M).

A steady climb on a clear stony trail leads to the windbreak on **Nan Bield Pass** (Wp.8 52M), from where wonderful views stretch away to the south along **Kentmere**, all the way down to **Duddon Sands** and the **Piel Castle** fortifications on the peninsula below **Barrow in Furness**.

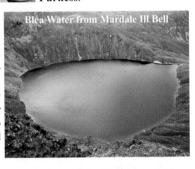

Blea Water from Mardale Ill Bell

Bearing right, we continue climbing on a broad eroded trail, generally on a relatively gentle gradient interleaved with one or two steeper sections (W then NW), forking left at a Y-junction (Wp.9 64M) and following the cairns for the final gentle northerly ascent to the summit cairn on **Mardale Ill Bell** (Wp.10 71M).

The main trail climbs directly to **High Street** summit, but in order to follow a bit of the Roman road, we head west, off-path, toward **Thornthwaite Crag**, unmistakable with its distinct beacon silhouetted against the skyline. 275 yards from **Mardale Ill Bell**, we join a clear path beaten out by walkers doing the classic **Kentmere Horseshoe**. We reach the **Horseshoe Path** just short of a narrow grassy way linking it with the main trail to the north (Wp.11 76M). We follow the **Horseshoe Path** for 400 yards before forking right at a Y-junction a few hundred yards from the scar marking the main watershed feeding the **River Kent** (Wp.12 83M). Following a broad way partially defined by a pronounced groove engraved in the peat, we climb to the corner of two walls, 25 yards beyond which is the broad track of the Roman road (Wp.13 90M).

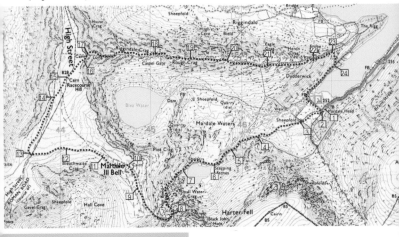

To climb directly to the **High Street** trig point, we should stay on the nearside of the wall running north-south, but for the sake of sentiment and a small historical frisson, I suggest going that extra 25 yards before turning right on the Roman road, which also happens to enjoy slightly better views to the west and northwest than the way alongside the wall. Presuming you elect to follow the Roman road, we climb gently (NNE) for 575 yards then, as the track approaches a smooth curving rise, bear right on a faint grassy path (Wp.14 101M) climbing (NE) to the trig point on **High Street** summit, sometimes known as **Racecourse Hill** for the derbies formerly staged here by shepherds (Wp.15 106M).

We now continue along the eastern side of the wall for 175 yards until a circular patch of erosion off to the right and two cairns, 75 and 100 yards from the wall (Wps.16 & 17 110M), mark the start of our descent; make sure you don't miss these cairns, or else you'll end up at **Penrith** with a sorry looking pair of sandals. Once we're on the **Riggindale** ridge though, there's nowhere to go wrong, so unless you care to pace progress, put the book away and just concentrate on the walking (which does require some concentration), and the great views over **Riggindale** and **Blea Water**.

The initial descent is badly eroded and rough underfoot, but we soon reach a more stable if steeper path, dropping down **Long Stile**, including one or two stretches where you may wish to steady yourself with your hands. Passing to the left of the tiny tarn on **Caspel Gate** (Wp.18 131M), we climb onto **Rough Crag**, the high point of which is marked with a cairn (Wp.19 137M). We continue along the rocky line of the ridge, dipping up and down, apparently heading for a sheer drop into **Haweswater**. In fact, the descent is relatively well graded, however, it does go on a bit, since every time you think you're nearing the end, another long, hitherto unseen stretch of the spur opens out below you.

After few hundred yards, our path suddenly drops down to a wall (Wp.20 147M), which we follow for nearly all the remaining descent. We soon cross a lateral wall and a small rise, from where we see the car park for the first time (Wp.21 153M). A steepening descent then leads to a chicane within sight of **The Rigg**, the wooded peninsula at the southern end of the lake (Wp.22 164M). A couple more chicanes break the final descent after which two large cairns and a breach in the wall mark the point where we turn right (Wp.23 169M) for a skittery, southerly descent onto the lakeside path (Wp.24 174M), which we follow back to our starting point.

GPS Waypoints for the walking routes included in Walk! Lake District South are quoted in British National Grid (BNG) co-ordinates for the Ordnance Survey GB Datum. Before loading waypoints into your GPS unit please read 'Using GPS in the Lake District' on page xx. To input the waypoints into your GPS set the 'position format' to 'British Grid' and check that your 'Datum' is set to 'Ord Survy GB'.

All waypoints are as recorded during Charles Davis' research, and are quoted to five figures each for **Easting** and **Northing** plus the two letters, SD, defining the OS map 'grid square' zone.

Full GPS Track and Waypoint files for these walking routes, plus all of our Walk! UK and Walk!/Walks Europe guide books, are available on our PNFs (Personal Navigator Files) CD version 3.01 available for £9.99 from Discovery Walking Guides Ltd. See our websites for more information:-
www.walking.demon.co.uk and www.dwgwalking.co.uk

1

SUNKENKIRK:
SWINSIDE STONE CIRCLE

Wp	Zn	Easting	Northing
1	SD	17886	85481
2	SD	18221	85348
3	SD	18181	85686
4	SD	18221	85865
5	SD	18424	86165
6	SD	18504	86270
7	SD	18567	86747
8	SD	18461	86716
9	SD	18377	86836
10	SD	18143	86969
11	SD	18069	87319
12	SD	17142	88169
13	SD	17241	87579
14	SD	17219	87131
15	SD	17447	86747
16	SD	17496	86588
17	SD	17363	86542
18	SD	17616	85809

2

BLACK COMBE

Wp	Zn	Easting	Northing
1	SD	13514	82702
2	SD	13056	82856
3	SD	13057	83243
4	SD	13074	83813
5	SD	13102	84926
6	SD	13407	85494
7	SD	13551	85490
8	SD	13587	85721
9	SD	13222	87012
10	SD	12295	87385
11	SD	11989	87588
12	SD	11756	87060
13	SD	11556	85408
14	SD	11750	84644
15	SD	12146	83619
16	SD	12561	82913

3

BURNMOOR TARN
& WHITE MOSS

Wp	Zn	Easting	Northing
1	NY	17640	01102
2	NY	17945	01493
3	NY	18171	01721
4	NY	18928	02203
5	NY	18891	02869
6	NY	18797	03776
7	NY	18612	03902
8	NY	18614	04184
9	NY	17901	03737
10	NY	17105	02730
11	NY	17140	02600
12	NY	17138	02455
13	NY	17297	02409
14	NY	17130	01583
15	NY	17649	01842

4

A RIVER ESK ROUND

Wp	Zn	Easting	Northing
1	NY	15287	00030
2	NY	15593	00036
3	SD	16102	99939
4	SD	16835	99993
5	NY	17170	00099
6	NY	17275	00052
7	SD	17426	99827
8	SD	17357	99557
9	SD	17386	99463
10	SD	17488	98856

Wp	Zn	Easting	Northing
11	SD	17631	98692
12	SD	17894	98109
13	SD	17373	97985
14	SD	17062	97695
15	SD	16261	96931
16	SD	15075	96830
17	SD	14084	96449
18	SD	13361	95909
19	SD	12963	95749
20	SD	12377	95745
21	SD	12014	95829
22	SD	11912	96070
23	SD	11740	96073
24	SD	11475	96088
25	SD	11041	96780
26	SD	10580	96370
27	SD	10347	96010
28	SD	09619	94939
29	SD	08403	96216
30	SD	08694	96500
31	SD	08902	95821
32	SD	09231	95706
33	SD	09796	96554
34	SD	09897	96898
35	SD	10043	96805
36	SD	10649	97629
37	SD	11053	98071
38	SD	11212	98309
39	SD	12061	98656
40	SD	12180	98942
41	SD	13137	99117
42	SD	13645	99341
43	SD	13929	99279
44	SD	14009	98928
45	SD	14675	99304
46	SD	14907	99505

5

GREENDALE TARN & MIDDLE FELL

Wp	Zn	Easting	Northing
1	NY	14436	05602
2	NY	14297	06125
3	NY	14323	06405
4	NY	14660	07328
5	NY	14700	07927
6	NY	14885	07995
7	NY	15074	07579
8	NY	15077	07220
9	NY	14902	06787

6

ILLGILL HEAD

Wp	Zn	Easting	Northing
1	NY	12846	03785
2	NY	12838	03698
3	NY	12944	03495
4	NY	13087	03289
5	NY	13192	03084
6	NY	13234	02982
7	NY	13319	02809
8	NY	13434	02398
9	NY	13514	02253
10	NY	13696	02350
11	NY	14020	02472
12	NY	14480	02696
13	NY	15107	03541
14	NY	15376	03825
15	NY	15861	04276
16	NY	16542	04800
17	NY	16906	05019
18	NY	17206	05160
19	NY	17654	05726
20	NY	18186	06196
21	NY	18346	07378
22	NY	18001	06872
23	NY	17689	06503
24	NY	16907	06107
25	NY	16419	05703
26	NY	15872	05208
27	NY	15425	04778
28	NY	15369	04660
29	NY	15267	04600
30	NY	15155	04454
31	NY	14616	03880
32	NY	14368	03752

7

GREAT GABLE

Wp	Zn	Easting	Northing
1	NY	18711	08544
2	NY	19257	09064
3	NY	19965	09277
4	NY	20396	09352
5	NY	20701	09420
6	NY	21272	09491
7	NY	21459	09503
8	NY	21878	09516
9	NY	21563	09933
10	NY	21415	10116
11	NY	21103	10309
12	NY	21036	10371
13	NY	20903	10520
14	NY	20769	10659
15	NY	20624	10439
16	NY	20439	09936

8

SCAFELL PIKE via ESK HAUSE & LINGMELL

Wp	Zn	Easting	Northing
1	NY	18068	07615
2	NY	18160	07557
3	NY	18522	07715
4	NY	18919	08174
5	NY	19380	08796
6	NY	19559	08938
7	NY	20620	09233
8	NY	21197	09126
9	NY	21363	09094

Wp	Zn	Easting	Northing
10	NY	21606	09053
11	NY	21873	09192
12	NY	22068	09261
13	NY	21986	09496
14	NY	22183	09457
15	NY	22661	09078
16	NY	22947	08677
17	NY	23138	08544
18	NY	23259	08115
19	NY	22598	07984
20	NY	22102	07561
21	NY	21736	07434
22	NY	21541	07213
23	NY	21447	07271
24	NY	21090	07449
25	NY	21078	07685
26	NY	21092	07928
27	NY	20933	08175
28	NY	20850	08379
29	NY	20304	08085
30	NY	20095	08044
31	NY	19850	07903
32	NY	19595	07849
33	NY	19238	07554
34	NY	19011	07349
35	NY	18715	07257
36	NY	18629	07224

Wp	Zn	Easting	Northing
6	NY	18683	08756
7	NY	18778	09037
8	NY	18239	10123
9	NY	18238	10427
10	NY	18399	10837
11	NY	18424	11080
12	NY	19171	11444
13	NY	18412	11663
14	NY	17769	11953
15	NY	17127	12104
16	NY	17033	11988
17	NY	16833	11763
18	NY	16561	11646
19	NY	16203	11464
20	NY	16214	11028
21	NY	16379	10794
22	NY	16533	10598
23	NY	16556	10144
24	NY	16702	09940
25	NY	16914	09800
26	NY	17298	09697
27	NY	17421	09361
28	NY	16947	08754
29	NY	16810	08124
30	NY	16800	07713
31	NY	16859	07370
32	NY	16666	07006
33	NY	17084	07063

9

YEWBARROW

Wp	Zn	Easting	Northing
1	NY	16772	06842
2	NY	16679	06998
3	NY	16861	07372
4	NY	16865	07448
5	NY	16892	07605
6	NY	16972	07700
7	NY	17008	07738
8	NY	17092	07782
9	NY	17227	08070
10	NY	17333	08472
11	NY	17607	09295
12	NY	17594	09405
13	NY	17597	09429
14	NY	17514	09499
15	NY	17366	09379
16	NY	16911	09115
17	NY	16722	08800
18	NY	16592	08456
19	NY	16592	08255
20	NY	16637	07723

10

The MOSEDALE HORSHOE

Wp	Zn	Easting	Northing
1	NY	18067	07615
2	NY	18152	07549
3	NY	18529	07717
4	NY	18920	08181
5	NY	18626	08351

11

SEATHWAITE TARN & The RIVER DUDDON

Wp	Zn	Easting	Northing
1	SD	22923	96141
2	SD	23153	96857
3	SD	23051	97148
4	SD	23255	97317
5	SD	23357	97362
6	SD	23657	97761
7	SD	23949	97855
8	SD	24308	98027
9	SD	24532	98208
10	SD	24945	98444
11	SD	25059	98802
12	SD	24839	98820
13	SD	24498	98716
14	SD	24308	98805
15	SD	24046	98864
16	SD	23788	99149
17	SD	23579	99259
18	SD	23637	99561
19	SD	23463	99580
20	SD	23324	99407
21	SD	23391	99247
22	SD	23346	98896
23	SD	23105	98114
24	SD	22937	97839
25	SD	22823	97549
26	SD	22787	97281
27	SD	22419	96377

HARTER FELL

Wp	Zn	Easting	Northing
1	SD	23488	99541
2	SD	23394	99668
3	SD	23017	99380
4	SD	22913	99180
5	SD	22805	99155
6	SD	22621	99178
7	SD	22507	99217
8	SD	22308	99288
9	SD	21995	99714
10	SD	21849	99709
11	SD	21751	99680
12	SD	21510	99463
13	SD	21136	99243
14	SD	21409	98857
15	SD	22192	98684

THE CONISTON FELLS

Wp	Zn	Easting	Northing
1	SD	22915	96176
2	SD	23164	96465
3	SD	23252	96500
4	SD	23432	96499
5	SD	23751	96868
6	SD	23979	96803
7	SD	24941	98454
8	SD	25093	98838
9	SD	25240	99549
10	SD	25787	99958
11	NY	26006	00357
12	NY	26588	00693
13	NY	27063	00090
14	SD	27119	99569
15	SD	27047	99346
16	SD	27076	98559
17	SD	27235	97827
18	SD	26621	98271
19	SD	26343	98169
20	SD	26253	97791
21	SD	26115	97085
22	SD	26081	96608
23	SD	25832	96472
24	SD	25079	96224

SILVER HOW, BLEA RIGG & STICKLE TARN

Wp	Zn	Easting	Northing
1	NY	31500	05387
2	NY	31842	05420
3	NY	32381	05586
4	NY	32710	05566
5	NY	32845	05704
6	NY	32527	05958
7	NY	32421	06152
8	NY	32266	06361
9	NY	31923	06614
10	NY	31863	06820
11	NY	31215	07126
12	NY	30904	07686
13	NY	30494	07680
14	NY	30326	07717
15	NY	30099	07785
16	NY	29622	08023
17	NY	28941	07741
18	NY	29008	07277
19	NY	29055	07029
20	NY	29588	06395

LINGMOOR FELL

Wp	Zn	Easting	Northing
1	NY	31497	05392
2	NY	30850	05762
3	NY	29925	06055
4	NY	29591	06044
5	NY	28757	05588
6	NY	28942	05121
7	NY	29308	05141
8	NY	29388	05327
9	NY	29691	05195
10	NY	29898	05017
11	NY	30125	04710
12	NY	30766	04296
13	NY	31144	04121
14	NY	31280	04168
15	NY	31222	04380
16	NY	32168	04576
17	NY	32320	04872
18	NY	32272	05196
19	NY	32187	05271

PIKE OF BLISCOE & CRINKLE CRAGS

Wp	Zn	Easting	Northing
1	NY	28612	06110
2	NY	28572	05792
3	NY	28548	05241
4	NY	28310	04688
5	NY	27946	04264
6	NY	27453	04200
7	NY	27306	04202
8	NY	27116	04213
9	NY	26685	03901
10	NY	25795	04237
11	NY	25130	04404
12	NY	25008	04559
13	NY	24914	04737
14	NY	24770	04902
15	NY	24973	05150
16	NY	24852	06031
17	NY	25465	06155
18	NY	26651	05833
19	NY	27294	05695
20	NY	27549	05620

A GREAT GREAT
LANGDALE ROUND

Wp	Zn	Easting	Northing
1	NY	28611	06132
2	NY	28532	06142
3	NY	29256	06479
4	NY	29212	06781
5	NY	28883	07059
6	NY	28812	07036
7	NY	28836	06843
8	NY	28207	07186
9	NY	27920	07323
10	NY	28178	07396
11	NY	27961	07988
12	NY	28077	09539
13	NY	27573	09177
14	NY	27133	09067
15	NY	26760	09040
16	NY	26592	08992
17	NY	26519	08683
18	NY	26188	08862
19	NY	25653	08333
20	NY	25407	08008
21	NY	24884	07748
22	NY	24575	07785
23	NY	24332	07885
24	NY	23438	08244
25	NY	23264	08112
26	NY	23529	07644
27	NY	23651	07500
28	NY	24078	07185
29	NY	24275	07116
30	NY	24472	06445
31	NY	24592	06345
32	NY	24704	06382
33	NY	24972	06067
34	NY	25306	05964
35	NY	25558	05735
36	NY	25907	05502
37	NY	25966	05396
38	NY	26340	05218
39	NY	26713	05224
40	NY	27625	05681

GRIZEDALE FOREST

Wp	Zn	Easting	Northing
1	SD	33560	94460
2	SD	33502	94759
3	SD	33223	94884
4	SD	33106	94882
5	SD	33068	94593
6	SD	33017	94603
7	SD	32609	95192
8	SD	32544	94685
9	SD	32596	94573
10	SD	32529	94335
11	SD	32734	93808
12	SD	32720	93740
13	SD	32786	93161
14	SD	32895	92692
15	SD	33014	92757
16	SD	33771	92463
17	SD	33911	92640
18	SD	33925	92747
19	SD	33953	93124
20	SD	33893	93359
21	SD	33763	93275
22	SD	33789	93651
23	SD	33756	93841

THE CUMBRIA WAY:
LOWICK BRIDGE to CONISTON

Wp	Zn	Easting	Northing
1	SD	29300	86514
2	SD	29225	86469
3	SD	28754	86503
4	SD	28508	86585
5	SD	28051	86789
6	SD	28126	86901
7	SD	27952	87120
8	SD	27842	87193
9	SD	27688	87100
10	SD	27349	87234
11	SD	27173	87349
12	SD	27186	87704
13	SD	27084	88204
14	SD	27428	88998
15	SD	27462	89145
16	SD	27667	91175
17	SD	27898	91373
18	SD	27961	91496
19	SD	28182	91620
20	SD	28120	91748
21	SD	28028	92192
22	SD	28811	92715
23	SD	29231	92848
24	SD	29768	94058
25	SD	29906	94303
26	SD	30075	94718
27	SD	30458	95877
28	SD	30391	96457
29	SD	30515	97252
30	SD	30156	97483

LATTERBARROW

Wp	Zn	Easting	Northing
1	SD	38566	99379
2	SD	38727	98885
3	SD	38748	97980
4	SD	38792	97621
5	SD	38781	97050
6	SD	38642	96446
7	SD	38415	96153
8	SD	38210	95944
9	SD	38211	96513
10	SD	38407	97127

11	SD	38088	97038
12	SD	38042	97207
13	SD	38204	97343
14	SD	38291	97437
15	SD	38230	97644
16	SD	37897	98039
17	SD	37733	98205
18	SD	37516	98632
19	SD	37323	98577
20	SD	36686	98807
21	SD	36720	99098
22	SD	36891	99316
23	SD	37166	99523
24	NY	37360	00052
25	NY	37615	00393

21

LITTLE LANGDALE via TILBERTHWAITE & HOLME FELL

Wp	Zn	Easting	Northing
1	SD	30291	97427
2	SD	30011	97598
3	SD	29429	98023
4	SD	29349	98161
5	SD	29283	98374
6	SD	29299	98490
7	SD	29341	98449
8	SD	29327	99078
9	SD	30039	99989
10	NY	29987	00658
11	NY	30636	01006
12	NY	30829	01405
13	NY	31193	01953
14	NY	31329	02056
15	NY	31586	02834
16	NY	31577	03365
17	NY	31862	03317
18	NY	31870	02835
19	NY	31841	02226
20	NY	31796	01960
21	NY	31890	01921
22	NY	31612	01364
23	NY	31586	01076
24	NY	31737	00887
25	NY	32007	00444
26	SD	32005	99819
27	SD	32013	99620
28	SD	32047	99455
29	SD	32026	99381
30	SD	31716	98911
31	SD	31501	98373
32	SD	31253	98258
33	SD	30705	98195
34	SD	30473	97811

22

A SWIRL HOW HORSESHOE

Wp	Zn	Easting	Northing
1	NY	30630	01021
2	NY	30544	01113
3	NY	30496	01201
4	NY	30421	01130
5	NY	30391	01251
6	NY	30106	01859
7	NY	30064	01943
8	NY	29956	01980
9	NY	29756	02094
10	NY	29533	02087
11	NY	29178	02002
12	NY	28758	01861
13	NY	28436	01881
14	NY	28481	02051
15	NY	28826	02410
16	NY	28884	02511
17	NY	28544	02544
18	NY	27448	02146
19	NY	26987	01365
20	NY	27056	01098
21	NY	27282	00548
22	NY	27820	00760
23	NY	28219	00940
24	NY	28821	01110
25	NY	28903	01193
26	NY	28991	01280
27	NY	29016	01350
28	NY	29190	01504
29	NY	29449	01651
30	NY	29643	01573
31	NY	30009	00769
32	NY	30271	00772

23

GRASMERE'S MENAGERIE: the LION, the LAMB & the CALF

Wp	Zn	Easting	Northing
1	NY	33638	07579
2	NY	33480	07692
3	NY	33444	07841
4	NY	32711	08441
5	NY	32687	08555
6	NY	32714	08628
7	NY	32647	08784
8	NY	32588	08951
9	NY	32784	08960
10	NY	32634	09351
11	NY	32450	09515
12	NY	31855	09922
13	NY	31052	10363
14	NY	30790	10305
15	NY	30474	10363
16	NY	30158	10414
17	NY	30111	10437
18	NY	29558	10281
19	NY	30074	09948
20	NY	31448	09654
21	NY	31770	09354

24

TARN CRAG via The Back Door

Wp	Zn	Easting	Northing
1	NY	33638	07579
2	NY	33501	07674
3	NY	33444	07841
4	NY	32710	08450
5	NY	32685	08556
6	NY	31769	09351
7	NY	30861	09806
8	NY	30205	09878
9	NY	30093	09924
10	NY	29990	09826
11	NY	30060	09571
12	NY	29999	09339
13	NY	30373	09300
14	NY	30388	09184
15	NY	30321	09110
16	NY	29904	09150
17	NY	29742	08899
18	NY	29654	08489
19	NY	29778	08462
20	NY	30088	08390
21	NY	30619	08448
22	NY	31023	08703
23	NY	31780	08744
24	NY	32447	08333
25	NY	33063	08165

25

STEEL FELL & SARGEANT MAN

Wp	Zn	Easting	Northing
1	NY	33636	07579
2	NY	33501	07674
3	NY	33445	07842
4	NY	33259	08093
5	NY	33422	09153
6	NY	33182	09601
7	NY	32970	09781
8	NY	32760	10107
9	NY	32603	10287
10	NY	32459	10498
11	NY	32165	10990
12	NY	32023	11163
13	NY	31942	11155
14	NY	31538	11296
15	NY	31436	11307
16	NY	30920	11203
17	NY	30560	11077
18	NY	30407	10929
19	NY	30161	10413
20	NY	30114	10445
21	NY	29556	10279
22	NY	29409	10044
23	NY	29277	09794
24	NY	29233	09423
25	NY	28946	09065
26	NY	28642	08897
27	NY	28995	08635
28	NY	29167	08418
29	NY	29653	08497
30	NY	30085	08394
31	NY	31027	08706
32	NY	31781	08750
33	NY	32460	08334
34	NY	33055	08156

26

LOUGHRIGG FELL

Wp	Zn	Easting	Northing
1	NY	34605	03982
2	NY	34734	04055
3	NY	34819	04124
4	NY	35193	04041
5	NY	35613	04341
6	NY	35466	04481
7	NY	35207	04555
8	NY	35140	04646
9	NY	34694	05141
10	NY	34506	05012
11	NY	34319	04892
12	NY	34420	04612
13	NY	34541	04532
14	NY	34715	04367

27

RED SCREES

Wp	Zn	Easting	Northing
1	NY	37606	04692
2	NY	37728	04687
3	NY	37759	05058
4	NY	37954	06736
5	NY	38205	08593
6	NY	38238	08887
7	NY	38335	09264
8	NY	38774	09506
9	NY	38994	09062
10	NY	39245	08700
11	NY	39425	08512
12	NY	39374	08411
13	NY	39217	08164
14	NY	39029	07552
15	NY	38821	07111
16	NY	38702	07007
17	NY	38664	06586
18	NY	38568	05348

28

THE FAIRFIELD HORSESHOE

Wp	Zn	Easting	Northing
1	NY	37604	04687
2	NY	37494	05445
3	NY	37637	06160
4	NY	37673	06624
5	NY	37468	07209
6	NY	37382	08060
7	NY	37402	08517
8	NY	37385	08922
9	NY	37453	10427
10	NY	36977	10982

Wp	Zn	Easting	Northing
11	NY	36922	11208
12	NY	36657	11414
13	NY	36369	11653
14	NY	35865	11729
15	NY	35581	10398
16	NY	35507	10196
17	NY	35672	08940
18	NY	35498	07464
19	NY	35592	07177
20	NY	35986	06871
21	NY	36176	06700
22	NY	36430	06492
23	NY	37171	05195

29

WANSFELL

Wp	Zn	Easting	Northing
1	NY	41172	02683
2	NY	41329	02805
3	NY	41240	02873
4	NY	41186	03364
5	NY	41113	03324
6	NY	40991	03349
7	NY	40493	03789
8	NY	40282	04066
9	NY	40377	04564
10	NY	40530	04991
11	NY	40317	05143
12	NY	40093	04770
13	NY	39825	04447
14	NY	39422	04165
15	NY	40129	04029
16	NY	40099	03660
17	NY	39902	03448
18	NY	39775	02404
19	NY	40146	02191
20	NY	40752	02644

30

ILL BELL & PARK FELL

Wp	Zn	Easting	Northing
1	NY	41209	02697
2	NY	41198	02580
3	NY	41613	02612
4	NY	41695	02722
5	NY	42081	03161
6	NY	42298	03546
7	NY	43485	04439
8	NY	43615	05342
9	NY	43622	06017
10	NY	43771	06739
11	NY	43659	07733
12	NY	43477	08098
13	NY	43517	08526
14	NY	43295	08838
15	NY	43183	08849
16	NY	42926	08141
17	NY	42838	07966
18	NY	42654	07390
19	NY	42575	06449
20	NY	42567	05901
21	NY	42349	05118
22	NY	42198	04758
23	NY	42139	04284
24	NY	41801	03184

31

A KENDAL ROUND

Wp	Zn	Easting	Northing
1	SD	51485	92627
2	SD	51751	91510
3	SD	51411	90967
4	SD	51220	90596
5	SD	51271	89980
6	SD	51171	89261
7	SD	50986	89310
8	SD	50635	89405
9	SD	50246	89360
10	SD	49822	89303
11	SD	49176	89066
12	SD	48843	88952
13	SD	48722	89343
14	SD	48487	89643
15	SD	48489	89894
16	SD	48861	90452
17	SD	48744	91314
18	SD	48663	91981
19	SD	48860	92388
20	SD	49238	92747
21	SD	49400	93878
22	SD	49919	93532
23	SD	50163	93324
24	SD	50755	93196
25	SD	50934	93065

32

WHITBARROW

Wp	Zn	Easting	Northing
1	SD	45131	89226
2	SD	44800	88847
3	SD	45030	88512
4	SD	44857	88023
5	SD	44928	87852
6	SD	45052	87702
7	SD	45465	86611
8	SD	45251	86491
9	SD	44734	86932
10	SD	44678	87646
11	SD	44519	87500
12	SD	44288	87498
13	SD	44186	87058
14	SD	43866	86919
15	SD	43719	87755
16	SD	44128	87920
17	SD	44605	88412

33

KENTMERE RESERVOIR

Wp	Zn	Easting	Northing
1	NY	45618	04121
2	NY	45921	04471
3	NY	45994	04630
4	NY	46046	04637
5	NY	46116	04644
6	NY	46248	05043
7	NY	46334	05353
8	NY	46393	05762
9	NY	45930	06312
10	NY	45254	06862
11	NY	44938	07128
12	NY	44727	07895
13	NY	44689	07635
14	NY	44898	06624
15	NY	45667	05947
16	NY	45676	04941
17	NY	45811	04400

34

HARTER FELL & HALLOW BANK QUARTER

Wp	Zn	Easting	Northing
1	NY	45610	04106
2	NY	45819	03987
3	NY	45951	04070
4	NY	46116	04083
5	NY	46234	04143
6	NY	47079	04635
7	NY	47590	04975
8	NY	47335	05351
9	NY	47241	06217
10	NY	47189	06703
11	NY	46668	07580
12	NY	46543	07783
13	NY	45862	08869
14	NY	45968	09325
15	NY	45750	09316
16	NY	45235	09593
17	NY	45037	08236
18	NY	45391	07654
19	NY	45617	07031
20	NY	46392	05736
21	NY	46339	05354
22	NY	46242	05035
23	NY	46113	04643
24	NY	45999	04630
25	NY	45904	04454

35

HAWESWATER RESERVOIR

Wp	Zn	Easting	Northing
1	NY	49928	15357
2	NY	48431	14032
3	NY	48114	13557
4	NY	47994	13136
5	NY	47908	11789
6	NY	46895	10680
7	NY	46737	10821
8	NY	47027	11130
9	NY	46795	11777
10	NY	47078	12653
11	NY	47063	13197
12	NY	47699	14446
13	NY	48680	15478
14	NY	50483	16143

36

SELSIDE & BRANSTREE

Wp	Zn	Easting	Northing
1	NY	46970	10748
2	NY	47383	11034
3	NY	47906	11788
4	NY	47959	11871
5	NY	48171	11925
6	NY	48330	11934
7	NY	48640	11915
8	NY	49491	12300
9	NY	49394	11873
10	NY	49342	11561
11	NY	49424	11253
12	NY	49079	11176
13	NY	48976	10893
14	NY	48334	10355
15	NY	47980	10182
16	NY	47800	09973
17	NY	47375	09301
18	NY	47033	09971

37

HIGH STREET

Wp	Zn	Easting	Northing
1	NY	46930	10716
2	NY	46884	10675
3	NY	46647	10563
4	NY	46155	10406
5	NY	45877	10255
6	NY	45678	10115
7	NY	45341	10028
8	NY	45232	09588
9	NY	44872	09843
10	NY	44760	10118
11	NY	44456	10189
12	NY	44007	10274
13	NY	43638	10242
14	NY	43922	10799
15	NY	44072	11044
16	NY	44225	11195
17	NY	44292	11264
18	NY	45033	11282
19	NY	45428	11247
20	NY	45840	11224
21	NY	46270	11171
22	NY	46807	11227
23	NY	47016	11314
24	NY	47024	11130

APPENDICES

Please note:

Telephone numbers are shown in red, and web sites /email addresses in green.

A ACCOMMODATION

ESKDALE
The Boot Inn 08451306224   www.bootinn.co.uk
Bridge End Farm Cottages, **Boot**
          08700 735328   www.selectcottages.com
Fisherground Farm
Campsite, Eskdale Green
          01946 723349   www.fishergroundcampsite.co.uk
(Fisherground has its own stop on the La'al Ratty narrow gauge railway)

King George IV, **Eskdale Green**
          01946 723262

WASDALE
Burnthwaite Farm Holiday Cottage and **B&B**
          019467 26242
Lingmell House B&B
          019467 26261
Strands Hotel, Nether Wasdale
          019467 26237   www.strandshotel.com
Wasdale Campsite   www.wasdalecampsite.org.uk

DUNNERDALE
Hall Dunnerdale Farm Cottages, Seathwaite
          01229 889281   www.hallsdunnerdale.co.uk
The Manor Arms, Broughton in Furness
          01229 716286
Oak Bank B&B, Ulpha
          01229 716393
Troutal Farm B&B
          01229 716235
Turner Hall Farm Campsite, Seathwaite

GREAT LANGDALE
Baysbrown Farm Campsite, Chapel Stile
          015394 37150
Old Dungeon Ghyll Hotel   www.odg.co.uk
New Dungeon Ghyll Hotel   www,dungeonghyll.com
Great Langdale Campsite   www.langdalecampsite.org

CONISTON
The Black Bull Inn
          015394 41335   www.conistonbrewery.com

The Coppermines Cottages
      015394 41765   www.coppermines.co.uk
Coniston Hall Campsite
      015394 41223
Lakeland Guest House   www.lakelandhouse.com
Low Wray Campsite   www.lowwraycampsite.org.uk

GRASMERE
Grasmere Independent Hostel   www.grasmerehostel.co.ik
The Harwood   www.harwoodhotel.com
Ivy Dene Guest House
      015394 35960
Oak Lodge   www.oaklodgegrasmere.co.uk
The Red Lion
      015394 35456   www.hotelslakedistrict.com

AMBLESIDE
Ambleside Backpackers   www.englishlakesbackpackers.co.uk
Low Garth B&B
      015394 34120 (day) / 34766 (eve)
Low Wray Campsite   www.lowwraycampsite.org.uk
The White Lion Hotel, Ambleside
      015394 31179

TROUTBECK
Fellside Studios
      015394 34000   www.bestofthelakes.com
Limefitt Campsite
      0870 774 4024   www.southlakelandcaravans.co
The Queen's Head
      015394 32174   www.queensheadhotel.com

KENDAL & KENTMERE
Ardrig Vegetarian B&B
      01539 736879

Garnett House Farm, Burneside www.garnetthousefarm.co.uk

Maggs Howe Camping Barn, Kentmere
      01539 821689

Pound Farm Campsite and Caravan Park, Crook
      01539 821220

Thorny Bank House, Skelsmergh - highly recommended
      01539 823671   www.thornybank.com

HAWESWATER
Bampton Post Office B&B
      01931 713314
Haweswater Hotel
      01931 713235   www.haweswaterhotel.com

ESKDALE

Egremont Castle
Hardknott Roman Fort
Muncaster Castle Gardens & Owl Centre
Florence Mine Heritage Centre (Egremont)
Ravenglass Roman Bath House (ruin)

Eskdale Corn Mill
Millom (en route) Folk Museum
Muncaster Mill

DUNNERDALE

Barrow-in-Furness:
The Dock Museum
Parkhouse Animal Farm

Furness Abbey

Dalton-in-Furness:
Dalton Castle   South Lakes Wild Animal Park

Grange-over-Sands:
Holker Hall and Gardens

Lakeland Motor Museum

Ulverston:
Gleaston Watermill
Lakeside & Haverthwaite Steam Train

Graythwaite Hall Gardens
The Laurel and Hardy Museum

CONISTON

Beatrix Potter Gallery
Go Ape - tree-top Adventure Park
Grizedale Forest Visitor Centre
Hill Top - Beatrix Potter's home

Brantwood (Ruskin's former home)
The Gondola Steamer
Hawkshead Grammar School
Wray Castle

GRASMERE

Dove Cottage   Rydal Mount

AMBLESIDE

Galava Roman Fort (Waterhead)
Stagshaw Garden

Hayes Garden World
Wray Castle

TROUTBECK

Townend
Bowness:
Amazonia World of Reptiles
The World of Beatrix Potter

Windermere Steamboat Museum

KENDAL & KENTMERE

Abbot Hall Art Gallery (Kirkland) Brewery Arts Centre (Kendal)
Heron Corn Mill & Museum of Papermaking (Milnthorpe)
Kendal Castle   Kendal Natural History Museum
Lakeland Wildlife Oasis (Milnthorpe)Levens Hall & Gardens
Museum of Lakeland Life & Industry (Kirkland)
The Quaker Tapestry Exhibition CentreSizergh Castle

HAWESWATER

Shap Abbey

C TRANSPORT NOTES

National and local public transport
0870 608 2608 www.traveline.org.uk.

National Express buses www.nationalexpressgroup.com

Cumbria has one of the best rural bus services in the country and the advantages of using it will rapidly become apparent when you're searching for a parking space at the start of one of the more popular walks on a busy weekend or fumbling about for enough change to feed the meter. An essential piece of equipment, even if you're arriving by car, is the excellent **Lakesrider** magazine, detailing **Stagecoach** www.stagecoachbus.com services throughout the northwest. The magazine is available in tourist information offices.

Mountain Goat minibuses 0153 9445161

Lakes Day Tripper tickets 08457 484950

For Walk 14
'The Langdale Rambler' 516 bus links **Ambleside** and **Dungeon Ghyll** between March and October, leaving **Ambleside** at 0720, 0900, 0950, 1150, 1350 and 1540, and **Dungeon Ghyll** around 25 minutes later. The last bus from **Chapel Stile** to **Ambleside** is at 1627. The weekend/public holiday services start and end later (Sat. 0900, Sun. 0950, last rtn. 1812), and are extended to include **Windermere** and **Kendal**.

D USEFUL INFORMATION

Tourist Information Centres:

Lake District National Park Information Centre at Ullswater
Beckside Car Park
Glenridding
CA11 0PD
017684 82414 ullswatertic@lake-district.gov.uk

Lake District National Park Information Centre at Keswick
Moot Hall
Market Square
Keswick
CA12 5JR
017687 72645 keswicktic@lake-district.gov.uk

Cockermouth Tourist Information Centre
Town Hall
Market Street
Cockermouth
CA13 9NP
01900 822634

Penrith Tourist Information Centre
Robinson's School
Middlegate
Penrith
01768 867466

Accommodation:
For accommodation listings, contact any of the above information centres or visit one of the many websites dedicated to providing tourist information for Cumbria. These include:
www.golakes.co.uk www.lakes-online.co.uk
www.lakesnet.co.uk www.keswick.org www.dokeswick.com
www.search-cumbria.com
www.virtualcumbria.net/accommodation

Cumbria Tourist Board also runs an accommodation booking line on 0808 1008848. To receive a holiday guide, contact the brochure line on 0870 5133059.

If you're having difficulty finding **accommodation**, try www.lakelandgateway.info/booking or phone for B&B/hotels at 0153 9434901, self-catering on 0153 9488785, or the Cumbria Tourist Board Accommodation Booking Hotline on 0808 1008848.

Weather:
For an up-to-date weather forecast for the Lake District, phone 0870 0550575. In the winter, this forecast also includes an assessment of the fell-top conditions, including depth, condition and likely locations of snow and ice, that is updated daily.

Mountain rescue:
To call out a mountain rescue team, dial 999 and ask for mountain rescue.

Fix The Fells:
The Fix the Fells campaign aims to raise £5 million for upland path repairs in the Lake District. To find out more or to make a donation, visit:
www.fixthefells.co.uk

Other outdoor pursuits:
For information on outdoor pursuits such as mountain biking, climbing, kayaking and para-gliding, visit:
www.lakedistrictoutdoors.co.uk

Other useful addresses:
The Lake District National Park Authority
Murley Moss
Oxenholme Road
Kendal
Cumbria
LA9 7RL   01539 724555   www.lake-district.gov.uk

Cumbria Tourist Board
Ashleigh
Holly Road

Windermere
Cumbria
LA23 2AQ   015394 44444   www.golakes.co.uk

National Trust (regional office)
The Hollens
Grasmere
Ambleside
Cumbria
LA22 9QZ   0870 609 5391   www.nationaltrust.org.uk

If you've enjoyed Charles Davis' writing, look out for his other walking publications:-

34 Alpujarras Walks	ISBN 1-899554-83-1
Walk! La Gomera (2nd Edition)	ISBN 1-899554-90-4
Walk! Mallorca (North & Mountains) (2nd edition)	ISBN 1-904946-19-4
Walk! Mallorca West	ISBN 1-899554-98-X
Walk! La Palma	ISBN 1-904946-06-2
Walk! Andorraa	ISBN 1-904946-04-6
Walk! Axarquía	ISBN 1-904946-08-9
Walk! Dorset	ISBN 1-904946-20-8

Published by:
Discovery Walking Guides Ltd.
10 Tennyson Close
Northampton (England)
NN5 7HJ

INDEX OF PLACE NAMES

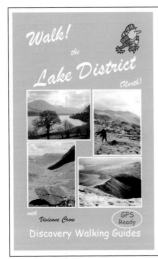

If you've enjoyed this book, try
its companion volume,
Walk! The Lake District North
with Vivienne Crow
ISBN 1-904946-15-1
published by
Discovery Walking Guides Ltd.

Walk! Wire-O Spiral Bound Guidebooks are designed to be used
with:

- DWG's plastic slipcover (PSC), which prevents the binding
  from catching on pockets and increases durability -
- - and our clear plastic All Weather Book Bag (AWBB) with
  grip-top seal which allows the book to be folded back
  displaying 2 pages, then sealed, impervious to weather
  conditions.

To obtain your PSC and AWBB for this book, send a C5 (9 x 7 inch)
SAE with 47p stamp, to:

(Code 978190494616X)
Discovery Walking Guides
10 Tennyson Close
Northampton NN5 7HJ